Know Your Customers !

How Customer Marketing Can Increase Profits

JAY CURRY

KOGAN PAGE

First published in 1991 in the Netherlands in Dutch by Management Press by, Amsterdam, entitled *Customer Marketing*, © Jay Curry 1991.

This edition first published in Great Britain in 1992 by Kogan Page Ltd.

Kogan Page Limited
120 Pentonville Road
London N1 9JN

© Jay Curry 1992

Copies of the spreadsheets are available in Lotus 1-2-3 and Excel for personal computers operating on MS/DOS, and for the Apple Macintosh. For more information, contact: Jay Curry, MSP Associates, Oranje Nassaulaan 53, 1075 AK Amsterdam, The Netherlands; telephone 31-20-679-3077; Fax 31-20-679-2224

British Library Cataloguing in Publication Data

A CIP record for this book is available from the British Library.

ISBN 0-7494-0751-4 PB
ISBN 0-7494-0844-8 HB

Typeset by Saxon Printing Ltd, Derby
Printed and bound in Great Britain by Clays Ltd, St Ives plc

Contents

Preface

Do we need another 'marketing'?

It seems we are confronted every day with some new form of 'marketing': action marketing . . . interactive marketing . . . database marketing . . . relationship marketing . . . non-profit marketing . . . and so on.

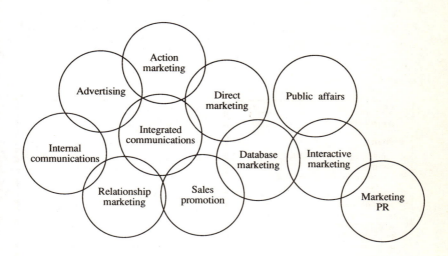

Figure 1

When you come down to it, most of these new 'marketings' have been invented by advertising and marketing services agencies trying to position their company uniquely.

And these 'marketings', based on a technique, technology or medium, are strongly pushed by the specialists in the technique, technology or medium.

If you want to increase sales, the sales promotion agency or department will tell you that sales promotion is the answer to a lot of problems. A direct mail specialist will generally recommend a mailing. And the PR man will suggest a 'media event' to generate press coverage.

It's simply human nature. The specialist earns his daily bread from his speciality – and doesn't feel comfortable outside it. In short, if the only tool you have is a hammer, every problem looks like a nail.

This kind of thinking often results in some smashed fingers: costly marketing and sales activities which don't work because they are based on inappropriate methods.

Isn't it about time to stop arguing about the kinds of technique or technology we use and concentrate on our marketing objectives?

Shouldn't the media and methods we use – and what we call them – be subordinate to our goals?

When you get down to it, companies are involved with only two kinds of goal-related 'marketing': corporate marketing and customer marketing.

Corporate marketing	Customer marketing
Objective: Convince people that the company is a worthy (potential) business partner.	**Objective:** Identify, acquire, keep and develop customers.
Targets: • employees • shareholders • government • trade colleagues • customers, prospects, suspects • etc.	**Targets:** • customers • prospects • suspects
Media and methods: Whatever are needed to reach the objective.	**Media and methods:** Whatever are needed to reach the objective.

Figure 2 *Corporate versus customer marketing*

Corporate marketing has the goal of persuading different

groups that a company or organisation is a worthy business partner. The groups include customers and prospects, of course, but also other key groups such as shareholders, employees, legislators, government regulators, local government authorities, people living in the neighbourhood of the company, competitors and colleagues, suppliers, etc.

Customer marketing is focused solely on prospects and customers. The goal of customer marketing is to identify, create, keep and upgrade customers.

Since corporate marketing and customer marketing are goal related, the question of which media and methods they employ is totally irrelevant. Both corporate and customer marketers can use the techniques and technologies of direct marketing, sales promotion, PR, personal sales, or whatever.

For instance, a distributor of high-tech gear recently told me that he raised 'brand awareness' in his market sector from 0 to 40 per cent simply by sending mailings to his prospects and suspects. No full colour, two-page advertisements were needed for this successful corporate marketing campaign.

Corporate marketing is an essential activity for every business. So is customer marketing. And that's what this book is all about.

Acknowledgements

This book would not have been possible without the help and support of:

- the clients (customers!) which I have been honoured to serve – and learn from;
- my partners Wil Wurtz, for helping me juggle the critical success factors, and Maurice de Hond, for the concept of customer marketing ratings;
- the stars on the 'Direct Marketing Borscht Circuit' – Murray Raphel, Robert Liederman and Ray Considine – whose concepts, ideas and presentation styles have inspired me over the years;
- Ed McLean, the guy who got me into the business;
- Magi Steinberger, for her comments on the final copy; and
- Yolanda Curry-van Berge Henegouwen, who has had to put up with being a night-time 'computer widow' while this manuscript was in development.

Any faults or omissions are the sole responsibility of the author.

Amsterdam, February 1992

Part 1:

Introduction to Customer Marketing

Chapter 1

What Business Are You In?

Has a consultant ever asked you this simple but profound question? If so, he may have been trying to appear wise and all-knowing. But more likely he was trying to see if you are *product orientated* or *market orientated*.

If you answer the question, 'What business are you in?' in relation to your primary product or service:

We sell shoes.
We are accountants.
We build houses.

you probably are rather product orientated. And this can be dangerous.

As Theodore Levitt pointed out in his classic article 'Marketing Myopia', the presidents of American railway companies in the early 1900s, if asked, would have answered the question like this:

We are in the business of operating trains.

The result of this narrow, product-orientated thinking was that virtually every US rail company went bankrupt or faced serious problems because they missed out on the rapid growth of the airlines and the development of a sophisticated highway system as a way to get things and people from place A to place B.

For the railroads, a better answer would have been:

We are in the transportation business.

Another example is IBM. Thomas Watson, Jr, son of the IBM founder, tells in his recent book, *Father, Son & Co*, how IBM almost missed out on the computer revolution in the early 1950s. Many IBM-ers – including his forceful father – would have answered the question this way:

We are in the business of supplying punch card machinery.

The old-guard IBM-ers were making huge profits selling the machines which processed the cards carrying the famous 'Do not fold, spindle or mutilate' admonition. They simply refused to believe in the benefits of magnetic tape as a medium to store data, and computers to process that data. Watson Junior, hearing major customers complain about the costs of storing and managing millions of punch cards, realised just in time that IBM's answer to the question should be:

We are in the business of data processing.

By exploiting and developing computer technology as a better, faster and cheaper way to process data, IBM became one of the largest and most successful companies in the world. (And converted from magnetic tape to hard disk technology when it became more cost-effective as a storage medium.)

As these examples indicate, a market orientation is much healthier for you and your business in this fast-changing world. But this book proposes that you deepen your market orientation to the level where it all happens: *the customer.*

Your company's revenues, profits and market share – and your salary – come ultimately from only one source: *your customers*!

No matter what products and services you provide, be it bars of chocolate, computers, insurance or temporary staff – customers are the heart of your business. When you get right down to it, the one single thing a company needs to be in business is a customer:

- You don't need money to be in business.
- You don't need to have an idea to be in business.
- You don't need a shop, factory or office location to be in business.
- You don't need personnel to be in business.
- You don't even need a product or service to be in business.

All these things help, of course. But without a customer, you're not in business. If you have just one customer, you are in business. If you have a lot of *good customers*, you have a successful business. If your company is successful – and I hope it is – I'm willing to bet you have developed a solid base of good customers who do nice things like this:

- *Buy more from you – even if your prices are (somewhat) higher than the competition.*
  Obviously you can't swindle people and expect to get away with it. But think about that small grocery shop or clothes boutique where they know your name or the service is pleasant. Yes, you pay a bit more. But you keep coming back.
- *Recommend you to colleagues, family, friends.*
  There's no better promotional message than a recommendation from a satisfied customer. People talk about their experiences with suppliers, both good and bad. A recent study showed that data processing (DP) managers rate advice from colleagues as one of the most important sources of information for buying a system, and that more than 60 per cent of DP managers give advice privately to colleagues outside their own organisation!

  Imagine – the DP manager of Procter & Gamble meets the DP manager of Unilever at a computer conference. They don't talk about soap. They talk about who's doing what to whom in the DP community – and their experiences, good and bad, with suppliers.

  While a good customer will generate a lot of business for you, a dissatisfied customer can hurt you badly. Who was it who said: 'For every complaint there are ten other dissatisfied customers who didn't make the effort to tell you of their dissatisfaction? And since every dissatisfied customer gripes to an average of six people, every complaint represents 60 people who are walking around with a negative image of your company.'
- *Make you the 'standard' for the organisation or family.*
  What could be better than having the boss at your customer site sending out a memo to all employees: 'All (name your product or service) must be ordered from (the name of your company)!' Good customers write memos like that.
- *Try out your new products and help you to make them better.*
  Good customers are usually willing to invest their time and effort to help you develop and improve your (new) products and services. In the case of mainframe computers and sophisticated technology, customer involvement in

15

research and development of new products can be worth tens of thousands of pounds or more in man-hours and expertise. And the best part is this: *as customers become involved in your business, they tend to become better customers!*

- *Use your support, service and other facilities.*
  Service, support, training, add-ons. These often highly profitable products and services are usually offered to customers with whom you have a good relationship.

If you believe that good customers are so essential to your business, you can answer the question 'What business are you in?' with:

'We are in the business of developing a solid base of *good customers* for our products and services.'

Chapter 2
The Customer Pyramid

If having a lot of (good) customers is the key to business success, you will want to know how many of what kinds of customer you really have. One way to find out is to construct a 'customer pyramid' like this:

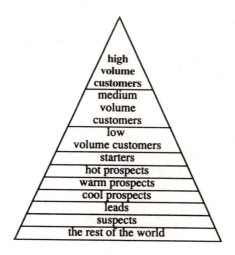

Figure 3 *The customer pyramid*

Take a list of your customers and rank them by turnover. Chances are you will discover that you have a customer base consisting of:

- a small number of *high volume customers* who give you a lot of business;
- a larger number of *medium volume customers;* and
- many more *low volume customers* who do business with you only once in a while, or at a low purchasing level;
- a number of *starters*, new customers, who may or may not turn out to be good ones.

Your customer pyramid may also contain prospects – people and companies with whom you are in contact, but they are not yet buyers. These prospects can be segmented into:

- *hot prospects* – people who are ready to buy, and you are on the short list.
- *warm prospects* – people who will probably buy in the short term, and you have a reasonable chance of getting the business.
- *cold prospects* – people who you are in touch with, but who are not ready to buy, or they have indicated that they are not happy about doing business with you.
- *leads* – responses from marketing activities which have not yet been qualified as one type of prospect or another.

To round off the customer pyramid, you may want to include the *suspects* in your market segment: people or companies who are likely to have a need for your products and services, but with whom you have as yet no relationship.

After that comes the rest of the world (where some suspects might also be lurking).

After completing this exercise, you may well discover the validity of the old 80/20 rule which says that 80 per cent of your sales (and profits) come from 20 per cent of the people you do business with – your good customers.

How can you get more (good) customers? That's what customer marketing is all about.

Chapter 3
Customer Marketing Defined

Simply stated, the customer marketing process involves:

1. Getting suspects into your customer pyramid;
2. Qualifying promising prospects;
3. Converting them into customers; and then . . .
4. Moving them up the pyramid!

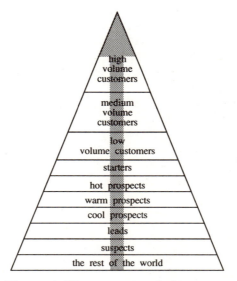

Figure 4 *The customer marketing process*

The result will be that you have more good customers. And, as we will see, the upward migration in your customer pyramid can give you explosive growth in profits – and increased customer satisfaction.

But to make it happen, you will need to use a solid base of information about your customers and prospects and a variety of methods and media.

Here is the 'official' definition of customer marketing:

Customer marketing is a *planned process* which uses a *customer database* and an *integrated mix of methods and media* to meet *measurable customer goals*.

The second part of this book covers the customer marketing process in detail. For now, let's look deeper into the other three elements of customer marketing:

1. Customer database
2. Integrated mix of methods and media
3. Measurable customer goals.

Chapter 4

The Customer Database

Customer marketing requires your company to be highly customer orientated. But a customer orientation is only possible if you have a lot of information about your customers and can communicate with them personally.

Let's see how a customer orientated shopkeeper uses customer information to improve his business.

Consider Mr Jones, a chemist in a small town. He knows a lot about his customers and prospects, having lived and worked in the town for years. And he has a sophisticated customer database system – right between his ears.

When Mrs Smith walks in, Mr Jones plonks down a prepared prescription and says, 'Good morning, Mrs Smith. Your monthly prescription is here waiting for you.'

'Thank you, Mr Jones,' replies Mrs Smith.

Mr Jones scans the Smith file in his customer database and retrieves some data.

'How is your husband's hip? Is it any better?' asks Mr Jones.

'Why, thank you for asking,' Mrs Smith responds. 'It's better, but not 100 per cent.'

Mr Jones pulls a box off the shelf and hands it to Mrs Smith. 'Why don't you try this out, Mrs Smith? We just got it in. A 16-valve, turbo-power hot water bottle. Costs just £19.99. It's supposed to work wonders. But if it doesn't, you just bring it back for a refund.'

'I'll just do that,' says Mrs Smith. 'Thank you very much.'

'You're welcome. Have a nice day,' replies Mr Jones, putting the money in his cash register – £19.99 in extra turnover.

Here is a classic case of upgrading a regular customer through use of information about that customer.

Of course, you can rely on your own memory if your customers are few and you have frequent and personal contact with them. But what if you have thousands of customers, and you don't meet them personally? The answer to this problem: your customer database.

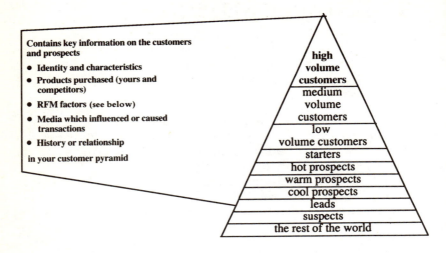

Figure 5 *The customer database*

Mail order companies, publishers, credit card vendors and other sophisticated direct marketers pioneered the development of customer databases running on large, expensive mainframe computers in the 1960s and 1970s.

Today, for less than £5,000 you can buy a computer and database package capable of storing and managing information on tens of thousands of customers such as:

- *Customer identity and characteristics.*
  Basic data such as names, addresses, telephone numbers are a must, but also characteristics such as type of business, number of employees, etc (for business) and sex, date of birth, family size, etc (for consumers).
- *Products purchased/requests/interests.*
  It is also important to store information on the products and services purchased or enquired about. From this information, you can deduce interest areas if you haven't already asked these via surveys or other means.
- *RFM factors.*
  Recency = when customer last bought.
  Frequency = how often they bought in, say, the past year.
  Monetary = how much they spent.

The concept of RFM factors was developed by mail order companies to segment their customer types. But the basic principle can be useful for all customer marketers.

- *Media and/or activity which influenced transaction.*
  You'll want to know which medium – be it a sales visit or a response advertisement – led to a sale or brought you the customer in the first place.
- *A history of the customer relationship.*
  If you get it right, your database will contain a complete history of your relationship with each customer and prospect in your customer pyramid.

Once you have this kind of information about your customers, you can also communicate with them on a *personal* basis with one goal in mind:

To create a strong link with your customers, just like the old-fashioned shopkeepers used to do, even if you have 1,000, 10,000, 100,000, 1,000,000 customers or more.

Imagine, for example, that you own a clothes shop and you have thousands of customers registered in your database. An analysis reveals that there are two types of women who buy baby clothes:

Type A: women aged 59–99
Type B: women aged 19–39

You use your brilliant mind to determine that Type A women are probably grandmothers or aunt types; Type B women are probably mothers.

Around 1 December you send a high-quality mailing featuring expensive and exclusive children's clothes to the Type A women, with a signed, 'personal' letter which comments that they have bought children's clothes in the past, and offers the collection as gift ideas.

'Thank you for thinking of me', say the Type A women, reaching for their cheque books while heading out of the door to visit your shop.

After the Christmas rush, you see what children's clothes are left over. You feature these items in an inexpensive mailing sent to Type B women as a post-Christmas sale of fine clothes at reduced prices.

'Thank you for thinking of me', say the Type B women, reaching for their cheque books, smiling secretly at the fact that they can buy the same items as their mothers-in-law a few weeks before – but at a 30 per cent discount!

Customer marketing makes people happy. Especially those who practise it.

And the same principles apply whether you're selling bull-dozers or baby clothes. But it will only work if you have collected information about your customers and prospects in your customer database, and can manage and manipulate the information efficiently.

An additional benefit of the customer database is accountability for marketing and sales expenses.

Who was it who said: 'We know that 50 per cent of all advertising expenditure is pure waste – but we don't know which 50 per cent'?

This kind of thinking is totally unacceptable to customer marketers.

If you record all transactions in your customer database, including the medium which stimulated that transaction, you should get a clear idea of how much value you received for all advertising and sales money spent.

Chapter 5

An Integrated Mix of Methods and Media

You hear and read much about 'integrated communications' these days. Usually that means some form of close coordination of a promotional campaign which combines advertising, direct marketing, sales promotion and publicity.

Customer marketing calls for the planning, registration and evaluation of *all contacts* between the company and its customers, prospects and suspects whatever the method or media: a sales visit, a direct mail shot, a response advertisement, or whatever.

The purpose of this integrated approach is to ensure that the most cost-effective medium and method can be employed for each customer or prospect situation.

As an example, let's say you are trying to get new customers for your fax machines. You can use your sales force to phone companies to find out if they have a fax; identify the decision maker; try to get a sales appointment; make the sales call; and close the deal.

You'll make some sales, of course. But given the high cost of a salesperson, and the limited amount of time a salesperson has (only 1,400 selling hours per year!), you will probably find that this mix of media and methods delivers more new customers, more sales and at a lower cost per sale:

- *Outbound telemarketing* to see if the suspect company has a fax; identify fax decision maker;
- *Direct mail* to the fax decision makers to generate sales leads;
- *Internal sales force call* to qualify the leads and make appointments for a demonstration;
- *External sales force* gives the demonstration, creates the customer, closes the sale;
- *Outbound telemarketing* to non-respondents; make appointment for a demonstration.

In the case of current customers, you can substitute some routine sales visits (costing £75 each) to regular customers with pro-grammed telephone calls (business calls) from the sales force (costing £5 each). The customer will appreciate the service, while the cost of the customer contact is reduced by £70. If the customer places an order over the telephone – which happens more often than you may think – the cost of the sale is a mere £5!

You can use virtually every kind of medium and method with customer marketing. But you may get yourself lost in a semantic jungle trying to distinguish between 'above-the-line' and 'below-the-line' media and joining the never-ending debates about the real meaning of 'direct marketing', 'sales promotion', 'advertising', 'marketing PR' and 'interactive marketing'.

To make life simple for yourself, categorise your selling methods and media into their degree of personalisation, like this:

- *Personal media and methods.*
  These involve two or more people communicating with each other who are – or become – personally acquainted.
- *Semi-personal media.*
  These involve an identified company representative who contacts a prospect or customer by name in the hope of eliciting a response which will develop into a (sales) dialogue.
- *Non-personal media.*
  These involve a message distributed widely to no specific individuals (suspects) in the hope that interested persons (prospects) will identify themselves by responding, thus leading to a sales dialogue.

As Figure 6 indicates, the more personal a medium is, the more effective it is – and expensive in terms of cost per contact.

A more detailed description of these methods and media can be found on pages 72–5 in Step 6. Select Methods and Media.

The integration of media and methods targeted on customers and prospects requires close coordination among the people involved and in charge of them.

- The *sales manager*, of course, runs the external and internal sales forces, and often has some control over the service staff, and telemarketing.
- The *marketing manager* usually controls the budget and activities for direct mail, advertising and promotions, and often telemarketing as well.

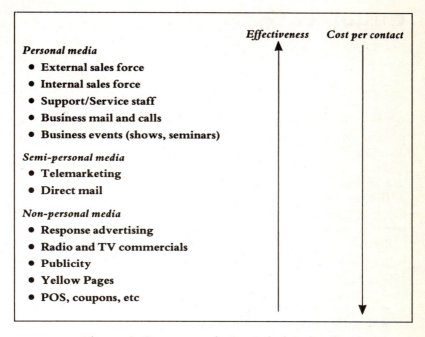

Figure 6 *Customer marketing methods and media*

Thus customer marketing involves some kind of integration – formally or informally – of the sales and marketing function. (It's not always easy to accomplish . . .)

Chapter 6

Customer Goals

What goals do you set for your company or business unit for a planning period? Market share? Profits? Profits as a percentage of sales? Turnover? Return on investment?

These are all tried and true managerial goals. And customer marketing does not neglect them.

But customer marketing recognises the inescapable fact of life that market share, profits, sales and return on investment come from only one source: *customers*.

Thus customer marketing requires you to translate your normal goals into *customer goals*, and specify how many of what kinds of customer you want to:

- identify (get prospects, leads)
- acquire (make a new customer)
- keep (maintain purchasing pattern)
- upgrade (increase purchasing)

for a given planning period.

Let's see how customer goal setting works in practice at Beancounter Publishing Ltd, a publisher of loose-leaf information services for accountants and financial managers. (*Note*. This example is based on real world data from an existing publishing company.)

Here are the basic figures for Beancounter Publishing Ltd.

Turnover	1,559,154
Cost of product	559,704
Gross margin	999,450
Total marketing sales	450,000
Contribution	549,450
Overheads	400,000
Pre-tax profit	149,450
Number of customers	4,953
Number of subscriptions	7,194
Turnover per customer	315
Subscriptions per customer	1.45

The staff at Beancounter decided to make a customer pyramid. It cost a few days with the computer, but here is what Beancounter Publishing discovered:

- 263 'Best' customers are good for £386,610 in sales, buying an average of 4.75 subscriptions providing an average £1,402 per customer in revenues.
- 1,276 'Better' customers deliver £719,957 in sales (average revenue £564, average subscriptions just under 2).
- 3,414 'One-Shot' customers – the great majority – subscribe to only one publication and deliver £510,587 in sales from an average revenue per customer of £150.

The staff at Beancounter made this customer pyramid based on this information:

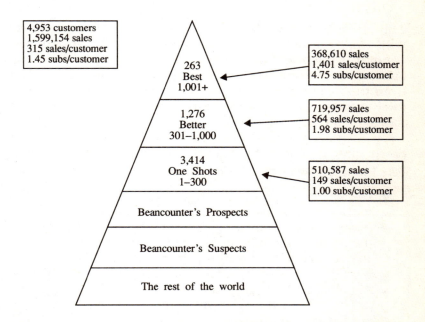

Figure 7 *Beancounter's customers*

And as the chart shows, 31 per cent of Beancounter's customers – the 'Best' and 'Betters' – are good for 68 per cent of Beancounter's turnover.

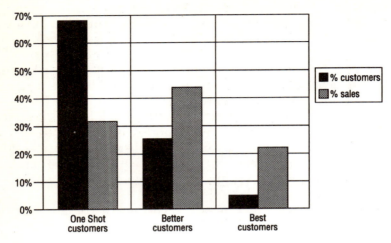

Figure 8 *Beancounter's customers and turnover*

Thus the bad news for Beancounter is that it has few customers with a high turnover, and many customers with a low turnover.

But that was also the good news! Beancounter has a working business relationship with a large number of customers. And from the Beancounter customer database, it can be seen who these customers are, what they buy, what they don't buy, what they should buy.

By reviewing spending patterns and discussing customer potential with the sales force, the customer goals for Beancounter Publishing Ltd were set as follows:

- *Upgrade* 400 'One-Shot' customers to 'Better' status and 40 to 'Best' status; 100 'Better' customers to 'Best' status.
- *Acquire* 500 customers (425 'One-Shots', 50 'Betters' and 25 'Best') from the pool of prospects and suspects to replace an expected natural drop-off from the customer base.
- *Keep* 3,913 customers (2,551 'One-Shots'; 1,099 'Betters' and all 263 'Bests') who are not candidates for upgrading, and not expected to fall away naturally owing to going out of business, dissatisfaction, mergers, etc.
- *Identify* 370 new prospects from the pool of suspects.

To make these goals clear throughout the company, the manager of Beancounter distributed this chart to all marketing, sales and editorial people:

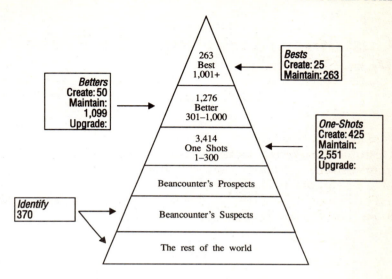

Figure 9 *Beancounter's customer goals*

What is the profit pay-off for Beancounter if its customer goals are achieved? The next chapter makes that clear.

Chapter 7

Customer Marketing: The Profit Pay-Off

Customer marketing seeks to create an upward migration in your customer pyramid. The result should be not just an increase in turnover, but an explosive profit growth.

For example, here is what Beancounter's customer pyramid looks like after meeting its customer goals:

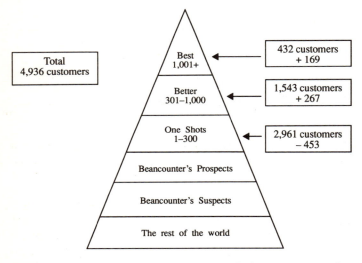

Figure 10 *Beancounter's customer pyramid after customer marketing*

Here we see the enhancement of the customer base by customer marketing:

- an increase of 169 'Best' customers
- an increase of 267 'Better' customers
- a decrease of 453 'One-Shot' customers.

More important, though, is the 'bottom line' impact on Beancounter Publishing Ltd. The chart shows it – a whopping 118 per cent profit increase – *despite a slight decrease (−17) in the total number of customers!*

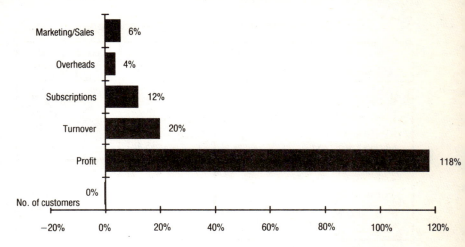

Figure 11 *Customer marketing: the profit for Beancounter*

How were these profits possible? Because the customer marketing profit pay-off is based on two facts of life.

> *Fact of life number 1. It takes much less time, effort and money to sell to your existing customers than to prospects and suspects who are not yet your customers.*

Take the personal computer business, for example. You have to work hard to make your first sale to a doubting prospect. It takes time – maybe three meetings and two demonstrations – to convince him that you understand what he's looking for . . . that you have the know-how and service capability in house to help him out when the system goes down . . . that you won't go out of business tomorrow. And all that time you spend with him costs money.

But once you've got him as a good customer, the second and subsequent systems purchases may require no more effort than accepting his telephone order.

Customer marketing profits are well known to book club operations. You've seen the advertisements: three books for only £5! It can cost a book club from £15 to £50 to get a starter, or new customer. But the following sales contact, via catalogues and mailings, cost only about £1 each. And assuming the member buys four times a year with an average purchase of £10 the profit is very interesting indeed!

Customer financials: Book club example

	First year	Subsequent years
Revenue	45.00	40.00
Product cost	11.25	10.00
Premium cost	5.00	0.00
Marketing cost	55.00	4.00
Total marketing sales costs	60.00	4.00
Total costs	71.25	14.00
Gross profit	− 26.25	26.00
Marketing ROI*	− 44%	650%

*Marketing ROI = Profit divided by all marketing and sales costs (investment).

Fact of life number 2. Good customers are more profitable than other customers.

The 'average' airline customer flies maybe twice a year to visit the folks at home. But 'average' can be the most dangerous word in business. My brother Ren, the rocket scientist, pointed out that if you add up all the people in your city, and make certain statistically valid calculations, you can come to the conclusion that the 'average' citizen has one breast and one testicle!

There are fewer than a million flyers in the USA who deliver more than 70 per cent of the profits for the whole air transportation industry: business people who fly frequently – and first class.

That's why almost every airline has a 'frequent flyer' programme to identify, create, keep and upgrade these highly profitable companies.

To summarise, customer marketing delivers profits because it puts your focus:

- on current customers, and thus reduced selling costs;
- on upgrading 'average' customers to good customers who are more profitable.

Figure 12 tells the story.

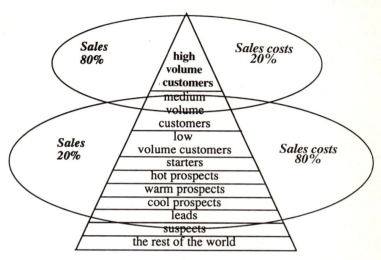

Figure 12 *Customer marketing: the profit pay-off*

Customer satisfaction: the extra profit of customer marketing

A second benefit of customer marketing is that it can stimulate – yes, even force – your employees to focus on your customers and satisfy their needs.

When you set customer goals, measure customer results and reward people based on these results, you can achieve more than any other kind of 'customer care' or 'quality circle' programmes.

Take the case of a bank branch office. The manager is usually evaluated and rewarded based on the total amount of deposits, loans and other sales. The other employees are usually rewarded on the basis of relatively subjective evaluations – and their customer service often suffers as a result, creating the need for 'quality training'.

But what if the bank manager and employees know that they will be rewarded by an increase in the quality and quantity of their customer pyramid?

You can be sure that the manager will focus his own and his staff's efforts on identifying, creating and maintaining customers. And there will be a definite improvement in customer service, because a lost customer means less reward.

35

INTRODUCTION TO CUSTOMER MARKETING

We have reached the end of our introduction to customer marketing. In subsequent chapters you will learn more about the customer marketing process, and how you might implement it in your business.

Part 2:

Ten Steps to Make Customer Marketing Work for You

Earlier in this book we defined customer marketing like this: Customer marketing is a *planned process* which uses a *customer database* and an *integrated mix of methods and media* to meet *measurable customer goals*.

We discussed customer goals, the customer database, and an integrated mix of media and methods.

Finally, we demonstrated the profit pay-off of customer marketing in terms of real money and increased customer satisfaction.

Could customer marketing play a role in your business? If you think so, or want to know more, this section describes the customer marketing process in detail.

You will learn a ten-step programme to introduce customer marketing in your organisation regardless of size. (*Note*. If yours is a medium or large company, I strongly urge you to begin customer marketing in one small business unit. Try it out on a small scale at first. You will make some mistakes and learn some valuable lessons before making any attempt to implement the process on a company-wide basis.)

To illustrate and demonstrate the customer marketing process, we will use a case: International Widgets Ltd (InterWidget). Although InterWidget is an industrial company with an external sales force, the basic customer marketing strategies and tactics used by InterWidget can also be applied by all kinds of business, including retail, financial services and even fast-moving consumer goods.

Customer marketing case: International Widgets Ltd

International Widgets Ltd (InterWidget) is a maker of high-grade widgets used in the machine tool industry. Here are its financial results last year:

InterWidget financial results last year

Turnover	3,642,544
Cost of product	1,827,571
Gross margin	1,814,973
Sales costs	601,950
Marketing costs	396,616
Total marketing sales	998,566
Contribution	816,407
Overheads	596,297
Pre-tax profit	220,110
Number of customers	866
Turnover per customer	4,207
Pre-tax profit per customer	254

InterWidget is not a world–beater, but at least it is showing a profit. Seeking to raise InterWidget's pre-tax profits to 10 per cent of sales, Bill de Vries, InterWidget's President, included these items in his business plan:

- increase sales by 10 per cent by recruiting 100 new customers
- hire another salesperson (+ £60,000)
- increase marketing budget (+ £40,000)
- keep overheads the same.

Achieving the business plan would produce the following financials for InterWidget:

InterWidget budget next year (traditional)

Turnover	4,000,000
Cost of product	2,000,000
Gross margin	2,000,000
Marketing/Sales:salespeople	660,000
Marketing/Sales: other	440,000
Total marketing sales	1,100,000
Contribution	900,000
Overheads	600,000
Pre-tax profit	300,000
Number of customers	966
Turnover per customer	4,141
Pre-tax profit per customer	311

But Bill de Vries discarded this plan. It would not result in the dramatic improvements he learned could be achieved by customer marketing, and he was uneasy about the investment needed in new sales people. So he decided to follow the ten-step customer marketing process.

Step 1

Capture Customer Data

Customer marketing makes effective use of information about your customers and prospects. So your first step is to pull together all the information on your prospects and customers which you have on hand.

You want to know who your customers are, their characteristics, what they buy from you, when they buy, how much they buy.

Even if you don't have a customer database up and running, you will discover you have in your organisation more data than you thought. Think about these sources:

- invoices
- contract files
- order forms
- service files
- credit applications/cards
- warranty and guarantees
- sales force reports
- general correspondence.

When you have exhausted your internal resources, you have to go outside to gather more information.

What is the best way to find out about your customers and prospects? The answer to this question is quite simple: *you ask them*!

It is amazing how much information customers and prospects are prepared to give you – if you just ask them politely, and provide a reward. Believe it or not, 70 per cent of all the people we asked agreed to spend half an hour with us on the telephone to answer all kinds of questions about their office equipment. Why? Because we showed an interest in them – and offered a free dinner, with a chance of a week's holiday as the grand prize. (The dinner didn't cost *us* anything either – the deal from the restaurant was one dinner free if one was paid for!)

Capturing customer data – the InterWidget case

It took InterWidget about two days of looking through the financial department's computer to come up with the names of customers and their purchasing patterns. But they still didn't know much more about the customers than their names.

To fill up their customer database, InterWidget conducted a postal customer satisfaction survey (with telephone calls to non-respondents) which asked customers to air any complaints and provide advice as to how InterWidget could improve their products and services. The survey ended with requests for information about the respondent's company, such as number of employees, turnover category, etc. It worked like a charm!

Step 2

Make Your Customer Pyramid

Once you have basic customer/prospect data you can define and quantify exactly what a customer or prospect is – and is not – and how to construct your customer pyramid.

Customer types by turnover

The simplest – and most used – method to define customers is simply by sales or turnover. Make a list of your customers during the last year, ranked by turnover in descending order. Then break out the top 5 per cent as the 'high' customers; the next 15 per cent of customers as the 'medium' customers; and the remaining 80 per cent as the 'low' customers. After that you add up the turnover per category and look at the results.

More often than not, you will discover that the top 20 per cent of your customers deliver about 80 per cent of your turnover.

You may also want to add a 'super' tier of customers by breaking out the top 1 per cent of your customers to see what they deliver. And here you may find out to your shock and surprise that a handful of customers may represent 25 per cent of your turnover – or more!

Customer types by RFM factors

Another variation is to define your customers by RFM factors:

- Recency – when did someone last purchase?
- Frequency – how often have they purchased within the past year?
- Monetary – how much did the customer spend?

For instance, a clothing retailer determined that the average family spends £2,000 a year on clothing and visits clothes shops eight times a year. He then defined his customers as follows:

	Recency (last visit)	Frequency (visits per year)	Monetary (yearly sales)
'Good'	within 3 months	four	£1,000
'Average'	within 6 months	two	£400
'Casual'	within 9 months	one	£100
'Starter'	within 1 month	?	?

Customer types by product purchases

You can also define types of customer by products or services purchased. For instance, in the insurance business, customers are often categorised as 'life' and 'casualty' clients.

Customer types by repeat purchases

If you produce capital goods such as large machines and cars, a more relevant way to define customers is by repeat purchases. For example, your 'top' customers have purchased a car three or more times in a row; a 'good' customer has purchased two in a row; and a 'starter' customer has bought a car from you for the first time.

Prospect types

A prospect is a person or company with whom you are in some form of dialogue or contact, and who is qualified to purchase your product or service: they have the money and the need.

It is also necessary to define and quantify your prospects in terms of probability that they will become customers, when and the amount of their order. It is only with this information that you can make reasonable business projections.

Most companies rate prospects using a three-tier system, such as A, B and C prospects. I have a personal preference for temperature – hot, warm and cool – to rate prospects something like this:

- hot prospect: 70 per cent chance of order and/or decision within 30 days.
- warm prospect: 50 per cent chance of order and/or decision within 90 days.
- cool prospect: less than 50 per cent chance of order and/or decision more than 90 days away.

Suspects

Some marketers also use the concept of a suspect. A suspect is a person or company which has all the earmarks of a customer or prospect, but you haven't yet made personal contact to evaluate their real need for your product and service, their ability to pay – and the chances that they will be doing any business with you.

Having analysed and defined your customers and prospects, you can now make your own customer pyramid.

Customer pyramid – the InterWidget case

After some experimentation, Bill de Vries segmented Inter-Widget's customer base into these customer types:

- Topper customers: purchase more than £10,000 per year
- Good Guy customers: purchase £3,000–£10,000 per year
- Low Boy customers: purchase £1–£2,999 per year
- Prospects: companies which had requested information or had been visited by a salesperson, but have not yet ordered anything from InterWidget
- Suspects: machine tool companies in InterWidget's territory with whom InterWidget has no relationship of any kind – yet

and made this customer pyramid for InterWidget.

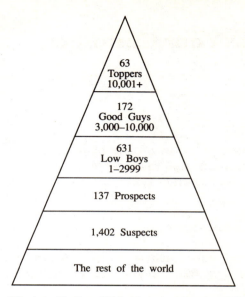

Figure 13 *InterWidget's customer pyramid*

Step 3
Analyse Your Customers

Now you have to build on the basic data used to make the customer pyramid and make a *financial analysis* and *market analysis* for each customer type.

Financial analysis

To understand what each type of customer means for your business, you have to get key financial data, such as:

- Sales: turnover after any commissions or discounts
- Gross margin: sales less direct cost of product
- Sales costs: costs of external and internal sales force
- Marketing costs: costs of semi- and non-personal media
- Contribution: gross margin less marketing and sales costs
- Overheads: all other indirect costs
- Pre-tax profit: speaks for itself!
- Sales per customer: average turnover per customer
- Customer profit: how much profit should be delivered by each (type) of customer
- Customer break-even: number of customers of each type needed to break even
- Return on marketing investment: what contribution was generated by the marketing and sales spend – including cost of personal media.

Take a careful look at the InterWidget financial data contained in the spreadsheets on pages 90–103 to see how you might structure your own financial information.

Once you have your financial data per customer type, you can make a more accurate budget and sharpen your financial planning to match spending efforts and activities to meet customer goals.

Market analysis

A market analysis of your customers – per type – should have two key kinds of information:

- *Customer share*. Customer share is the percentage of companies or consumers in your market (segment) with whom you do business. In addition to knowing where you stand versus competition, customer share data can help you to determine customer acquisition goals.
- *Customer characteristics*. Knowing the characteristics of each type of customer will help you to determine which customers are ripe for upgrading, and identify prospects and suspects you should target for customer acquisition efforts.

  In the business–to–business marketplace, common characteristics are type of industry, number of employees, total revenues. Other characteristics to look for in your customer base, depending on your business, may be very narrow or specific. For example, if you are selling training courses, your good customers will probably have a large training department and/or a training manager on the payroll.

  Consumer customers are often segmented by sex, age, house location, income level, education level, number of children, possession of one or more credit cards, etc.

Customer analysis – the InterWidget case

InterWidget financial analysis

Bill de Vries spent some long hours working on his spreadsheet, talking with the accountants and making some inspired assumptions. (For instance, he allocated marketing, sales and overheads equally across the prospect and customer groups because there was no way to do it differently.)

Copies of Bill's spreadsheets can be found on pages 90–103. They give you the details and show you how he set them up.

The first thing Bill de Vries discovered was that InterWidget was not immune from the 80/20 rule (80 per cent of turnover comes from 20 per cent of the customers). His Topper and Good Guy customers, 27 per cent of his customer base, were good for 74 per cent of the sales. Even more dramatic, these 235 customers contributed 94 per cent of InterWidget's profits!

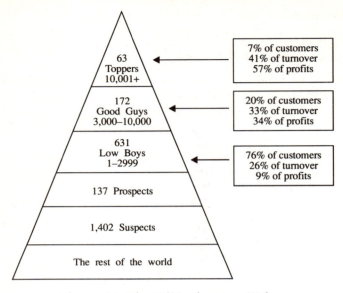

Figure 14 *The 80/20 rule at InterWidget*

Bill took a closer look at the numbers to find out why. And he discovered a major difference in return on sales and marketing return on investment for each customer type. As Figure 15 shows, the Low Boys delivered a 6 per cent return on sales versus 17 per cent on the Good Guys and a very nice 24 per cent for the Toppers.

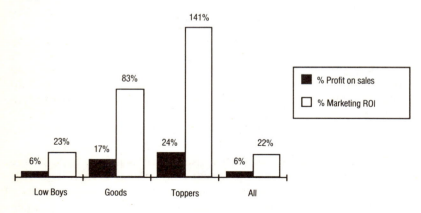

Figure 15 *InterWidget percentage profit and percentage ROI*

The difference in marketing ROI was understandable for Bill. But he was puzzled by the return on sales figures because InterWidget was doing about 6 per cent profit on return on sales for all customers. Why wasn't he getting a better return on sales?

Bill found the answer in his analysis of turnover and profit per customer type, as shown in Figure 16.

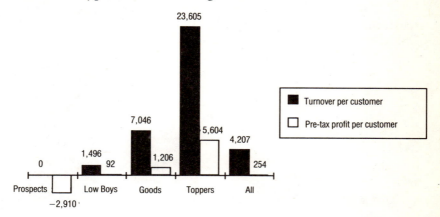

Figure 16 *InterWidget turnover and profit per customer type*

Here you see what Bill found out about the financial performance of his various customer types:

- 63 Toppers averaged £23,605 in turnover and £5,604 profit per customer.
- 172 Good Guys delivered an average of £7,046 in turnover and £1,206 profit per customer.
- 631 Low Boys – the great majority – were good for £1,496 in turnover each, with just £92 in profit per customer.

Most disturbing, however, was the fact that 137 prospects, with no turnover, were costing InterWidget £2,910 each in marketing and sales costs, plus overheads – a total of almost £400,000. The losses in the prospect category were cutting deeply into profits and overall return on sales.

Bill realised that he should be more careful about his marketing expenses on non-customers (prospects and suspects), and perhaps focus a bit more on the InterWidget customer base.

Above all, he concluded that InterWidget needed a lot more Topper customers. To find out where to get them, he carried out his market analysis.

InterWidget market analysis

Bill first made an analysis of his customer base to determine the characteristics of his customers based on the information InterWidget collected with the customer satisfaction survey. They key characteristic he focused on was the size of customers expressed in number of employees.

As Figure 17 shows, slightly more than half of InterWidget's customers were small companies. And only 5 per cent had more than 500 employees.

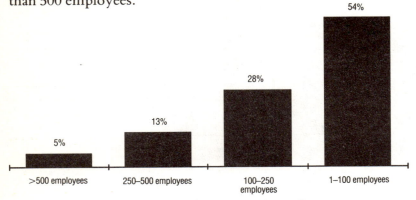

Figure 17 *The InterWidget customer base: all customers*

Looking deeper, Bill de Vries confirmed his own intuition that his best customers (Toppers) tended to be the larger machine tool manufacturers. But surprisingly, there were a number of very small companies among the Toppers – and some large companies who were Low Boys and clearly prospects for upgrading!

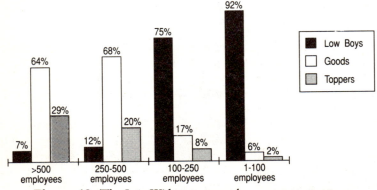

Figure 18 *The InterWidget customer base per customer type*

Bill then looked at his customer base against the entire market of machine tool manufacturers in his area. As Figure 19 reflects, the InterWidget customer base had proportionally twice as many larger companies than the market:

- 5 per cent of InterWidget customers had 500 employees versus 2 per cent for the market.
- 13 per cent of InterWidget customers had 250–500 employees as against 6 per cent for the market.

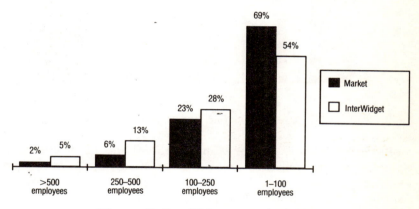

Figure 19 *InterWidget versus the market*

Continuing his market analysis, Bill took a look at his non-customers – the InterWidget prospects and suspects.

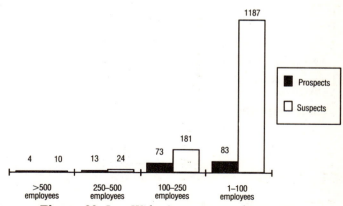

Figure 20 *InterWidget's prospects and suspects*

From this information, Bill calculated InterWidget's customer share – the percentage of companies of each machine tool manufacturer in the marketplace he could count as his customers. He found that he had an overall 34 per cent customer share. But among the larger companies, his customer share was 75 per cent.

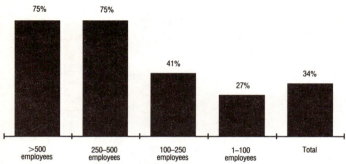

Figure 21 *The InterWidget customer share*

Bill de Vries knew that he wanted more Toppers. But he was already doing business with the great majority of larger companies in his area. Thus he concluded that the most likely source of the additional Topper customers he wanted were *already present in his existing customer base*!

And he vowed to move these customers up into the top of his customer pyramid by following the customer marketing strategy.

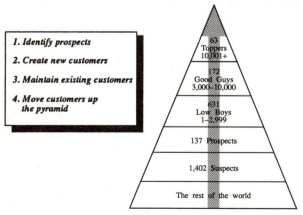

Figure 22 *The InterWidget strategy*

The next step was to set specific goals for identifying, creating, maintaining and upgrading InterWidget customers.

Set Customer Goals

Customer goal setting is the most critical – and often the most difficult – step in customer marketing.

It is possible to set customer goals through rough guesstimates. And, indeed, you will have to make some decisions based on intuition, sales force estimates – with a bit of wishful thinking thrown in for good measure.

But since you will be setting specific goals, and measuring results, you should try to base your customer goals on a combination of statistical probabilities plus human input. And this we call *customer marketing ratings*.

Customer marketing ratings

The customer marketing rating is a numeric score for each customer, prospect and suspect to indicate where that company or individual 'belongs' in your customer pyramid. It is a combination of a *statistical score*, based on pure analysis of data, and a *contact score*, based on input provided by someone with knowledge of the customer, prospect or suspect.

As an example, let's take a law firm (yes, law firms have also put customer marketing concepts to good use!), which had created a customer pyramid with High, Medium and Low customers based on turnover. Using a scale from 1 to 10, the law firm assigned customer marketing ratings to these *prospect* categories:

Potential to be a High customer	18 or 19
Potential to be a Medium customer	15 to 17
Potential to be a Low customer	10 to 14

and to these *customer* categories:

Potential to be a High customer	28 or 29
Potential to be a Medium customer	25 to 27
Potential to be a Low customer	20 to 24

Statistical scores

As mentioned earlier, the common characteristics of your various customer types provide the basis for setting customer goals. When you are dealing with many characteristics and variables, you can get into the higher mathematical ground of regression analysis.

But often you can keep it simple. The law firm analysed its clients by industry sector and discovered, among other things, that large banks made up a high percentage of its top customers, and small retail stores formed the basis of its low-end customers.

Accordingly, *bank prospects* were assigned a statistical score, depending on their assets, from 18 or 19 and *bank customers* statistical scores of 28 or 29. Small retail stores, depending on their turnover, were allocated statistical scores of 10 to 14 for *prospects* and statistical scores of 20 to 24 for *customers*.

During the yearly exercise of developing, the law firm assigned to prospect Bank B a statistical score of 18. A retail customer, Retailer R, was given a statistical score of 22.

Contact scores

But a statistical score should be supplemented whenever possible with direct, up-to-date information based on the 'real world', such as the assessment of a salesperson or someone who has direct contact with or knowledge of the customer, prospect or suspect. And this knowledge can be converted into a *contact score*.

Obviously, contact scores cannot be used in the case of suspects with which there has been no contact or of whom there is no knowledge. In these instances your customer marketing rating will be solely on the statistical score – unless you decide to contact key suspects to provide information for a contact score, and thus turn them into prospects!

A contact score may be given a heavier weighting than the statistical score because the 'real world' input by the salespeople may be more accurate. But the statistical score provides a useful check against the subjective assessments of the sales force who, being human, sometimes allocate low contact scores to cover their own shortcomings.

In fact, if you have no statistical score you can still assign customer marketing ratings purely on contact scores with some success.

Let's see how the contact scores were applied in the law firm example.

A lawyer familiar with Bank B knew that the brother-in-law of Bank B's president was a senior partner in a competing law firm. Thus he gave Bank B a contact score of 11, because he judged that the law firm was only likely to get small assignments – if ever.

And another lawyer gave Retailer R a contact score of 28. Why? Because he knew that the retailer had just inherited millions, and was planning to undertake an expansion programme involving the take-over of a large number of shops, thereby generating a lot of legal fees!

By averaging the statistical scores and contact scores, the law firm arrived at these customer marketing ratings:

Customer marketing rating for Bank B = 14.5
(Average of statistical score of 18 and contact score of 11)

Customer marketing rating for Retailer R = 15
(Average of statistical score of 12 and contact score of 18)

Once you know from customer marketing ratings where customer, prospect and suspect 'belong' in your pyramid, you can estimate your chances of getting them there based on past experiences and the marketing and sales resources you will allocate to the effort.

Then you are in a position to answer these critical questions:

1. *Identification goals.* How many suspects in our pool can we convert to a prospect in the planning period?
2. *Creation goals.* Which suspects and prospects can we turn into what types of customer in the planning period?
3. *Maintenance goals.* Which customers can we maintain at current purchasing levels in the planning period?
4. *Upgrading goals.* Which customers can we move up the pyramid to a higher status in the planning period?

You then simply add or subtract the number of prospects and customers in your customer pyramid based on the answers to the above questions. Hey presto! You've got your customer goals!

Alternatively, you can match your customer goals to your business goals. If you want 10 per cent more turnover – or 20 per cent more margin – what kind of customer portfolio do you need to reach those goals?

Tip. It's not a bad idea to be a bit conservative at first – and don't forget to discount the number of customers who might drop down in spending, or disappear from view.

Setting customer goals – the InterWidget case

Bill de Vries decided to base his customer marketing ratings on the key factor which appeared to determine the potential of customers and prospects: the size of the customer in terms of personnel. To this information would be added the assessment of his sales representatives.

InterWidget statistical scores

To keep things simple, Bill simply matched statistical scores for *prospects*' with the number of employees, and allocated scores for the prospects' potential based on his analysis of the InterWidget customers. The statistical score for prospects ranged from 1 to 900. A prospect from 1 to 399 employees was judged to be a Low Boy candidate; from 400 to 599 a Good Guy candidate; and above 600 a Topper candidate.

InterWidget statistical score: prospects and suspects

Number of employees	Statistical score	Type of customer candidate
900 or more	900	Topper
800–899	800–899	Topper
700–799	700–799	Topper
600–699	600–699	Topper
500–599	500–599	Good Guy
400–499	400–499	Good Guy
300–399	300–399	Low Boy
200–299	200–299	Low Boy
100–199	100–199	Low Boy
1– 99	1– 99	Low Boy

Statistical scores for *customers* were based on the same basic structure, but started with a lowest score of 1,001 and a highest score of 1,900.

InterWidget statistical score: customers

Number of employees	Statistical score	Type of customer candidate
900 or more	1,900	
800–899	1,800–1,899	
700–799	1,700–1,799	Topper
600–699	1,600–1,699	
500–599	1,500–1,599	Good Guy
400–499	1,400–1,499	
300–399	1,300–1,399	
200–299	1,200–1,299	Low Boy
100–199	1,100–1,199	
1– 99	1,001–1,099	

InterWidget contact scores

Bill kept the same point system for the InterWidget contact scores. But he decided to weight the contact scores by a factor of 2 since he felt that his sales force was well equipped to evaluate the real potential of a prospect or customer.

InterWidget contact score: prospects and suspects

Contact score (weighting 2×)	Type of customer candidate
Between 600 and 900	Topper
Between 400 and 599	Good Guy
Between 1 and 399	Low Boy

InterWidget contact score: customers

Contact score (weighting 2×)	Type of customer potential
Between 1,600 and 1,900	Topper
Between 1,400 and 1,599	Good Guy
Between 1,001 and 1,399	Low Boy

InterWidget customer marketing ratings

As the following indicate, InterWidget's customer marketing ratings were arrived at by adding the statistical score plus 2 times the contact score and dividing by 3.

InterWidget customer marketing rating: prospects and suspects

CM rating (SS+CS+CS)/3	Type of customer candidate
Between 600 and 900	Topper
Between 400 and 599	Good Guy
Between 1 and 399	Low Boy

InterWidget customer marketing rating: customers

CM rating (SS+CS+CS)/3	Type of customer candidate
Between 1,600 and 1,900	Topper
Between 1,400 and 1,599	Good Guy
Between 1,001 and 1,399	Low Boy

To implement the rating system, Bill had rating cards made up for each customer and prospect on which he put:

- The name of the prospect or customer.
- The date when scores were to be completed.
- The number of employees.
- The current place of the prospect or customer in the InterWidget customer pyramid.
- The statistical score, based on number of employees.

These cards were handed out to the sales force after a briefing on the system, with instructions for them to:

- Add a contact score.
- Calculate the customer marketing rating.
- Indicate the potential position in the pyramid.
- Write down the customer goal required to get the prospect or customer in that position.
- Estimate the chance of reaching that goal.

The cards looked like this:

InterWidget customer marketing rating card for prospects and suspects

Ajax Machine Tools Inc No. of employees: 325	
Current status:	Hot Prospect
Statistical score:	325
Contact score:	450
CM rating:	408
CM goal:	Create
Type:	Good Guy
Chance:	50%

InterWidget customer marketing rating card for customers

Eurotool Ltd No. of employees: 435	
Current status:	Low Boy
Statistical score:	1,435
Contact score:	1,850
CM rating:	1,712
CM goal:	Upgrade
Type:	Topper
Chance:	75%

Bill discovered that getting his salespeople involved in assigning customer marketing ratings for prospects and customers turned out to be highly motivating, and led to a better understanding of – and commitment to – customer marketing as the InterWidget way of doing business.

On the basis of these customer marketing ratings – and taking into consideration that they might lose 115 customers in the coming year owing to closures, mergers, bankruptcies, etc – Bill de Vries set these customer goals for InterWidget:

- Identification goals
  – identify 140 new prospects from the pool of suspects.
- Creation goals
  – 70 Low Boy customers
  – 15 Good Guy customers
  – 5 Topper customers
- Maintenance goals
  – 564 Low Boys
  – 172 Good Guys
  – 63 Toppers
- Upgrading goals
  – 67 Low Boys (42 to Good Guy status; 25 to Topper status)
  – 35 Good Guy to Topper status.

To make sure that everyone at InterWidget was aware of the company's customer goals, he compiled and distributed this pyramid chart to all staff:

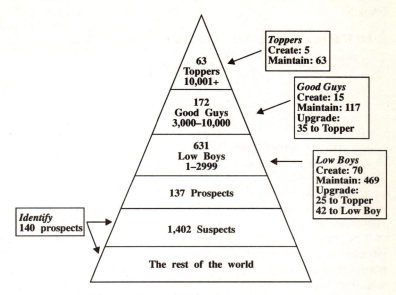

Figure 23 *InterWidget's customer goals*

Develop a Customer Benefits Package

Once your customer goals are set, you must start thinking about developing a customer benefits package to help you reach them.

A customer benefits package is a cluster of services and rewards – in addition to your normal products and services – which you will offer to new and existing customers to help you meet your customer goals.

Take your time over this important step. Your customer benefits package may be the only factor which distinguishes you from your competitors. As such, it could be the primary reason why people will become your customers – and remain so.

The goodies in the customer benefits package need not be expensive. But the benefits must have a perceived rational or emotional value for the prospect when you promise them – and the benefits must provide satisfaction when you deliver them.

Benefits to identify potential customers

These benefits must be designed to get prospective customers to identify themselves to you as people or companies interested in your products and services.

For instance, if you are selling fancy CD players, you might want to develop a booklet 'Checklist for Selecting Your Next CD'. You can then offer this benefit free via an advertisement in a special interest magazine, *CD News*. Anyone ordering the booklet is most likely to be interested in your products – and he supplies you with his name, address and telephone number on the coupon.

Examples of commonly used benefits which encourage prospects to identify themselves to you include:

- Free (or almost free) booklet
- Free (or almost free) seminar
- Free (or almost free) sample

- Sweepstakes and games requiring a response
- Free (or almost free) gifts and premiums requiring a trial purchase.

Benefits to create new customers

You often have to offer a major benefit to stimulate people to start doing business with you on a regular basis and become your customer.

Book clubs, for instance, offer three books for only £6. But the new customer makes a commitment to buy four additional books within a year – and more than 90 per cent keep this promise.

Discount benefits

Many companies offer a 'starter' or 'get acquainted' discount to find new customers. The main advantage of a discount benefit is that it takes no time or energy to develop. The disadvantage is that discounts can dilute the perceived quality of your products or weaken your pricing structure.

I prefer to offer a free accessory, premium or service with perceived value, rather than giving a discount on the main product. Credit cards, for instance, waive the £50 entry fee but give no discount on the yearly membership fee. And machinery suppliers can offer the first six months of a service contract free.

'Member–get–member' and reference benefits

Your satisfied customers should be your best source of new customers. There is simply no stronger form of promotion than a recommendation from a satisfied customer. If you have satisfied customers, you will get new business from their recommendations. But why not stimulate and structure that process?

The shop which sold me a waterbed sent me an offer of a chance to win a free weekend away if I introduced a new prospect. They provided me with a special 'courtesy card' to give to family or friends to introduce them to the shop.

You can try the same thing, but also consider giving the same premium to both the existing and the new prospect.

In the business–to–business area, a classical 'member–get–member' activity may seem out of place. But there is nothing wrong in asking current customers for referrals for new business – and rewarding these referrals with an appropriate gesture, such as a special Christmas gift at the end of the year or a certificate for a dinner at a fancy restaurant for the customer and his partner.

Benefits to maintain customers

Customer marketing recognises this fact of business life:

> *Almost every business owes its existence to a regular flow of orders from regular customers. But many – if not most – marketing and sales managers devote the majority of their time – and budgets – to trying to get new customers!*

The result: regular customers become neglected. Or are left to cope with the not-always-customer-friendly departments in the company: accounts, production, technical service, etc.

Take the credit card business, for instance. You receive a personal letter signed by the managing director in the post designed to enlist you as a customer.

But once you become a customer, the personal letter from the managing director is replaced by monthly statements which sometimes contain threats about your late payment spewed by an anonymous 'Big Brother' computer, all in hard-to-read capital letters.

If you are treated this way, you may well be willing to respond to an offer from a competitive credit card company, hoping that they will treat you better as a regular customer.

Regular benefits and recognition for steady customers

So think hard about what benefits you want to offer your regular customers. They need not be expensive rewards, but rather gestures which recognise your appreciation for their business.

In all fairness, I must tell you about Diners Club which sent me a card on my birthday and a reward of 500 bonus points on their incentive scheme. (The next year, they coupled the birthday card with a wine offer – paid for, no doubt, by the vineyard!)

Why not send a 'birthday card' to your customers on the anniversary date of their first purchase or order?

Here are some other regular benefits you can offer steady customers – to keep them steady:

- Publications and 'magalogues'.

- Credit facilities or a credit card.
- Free Hotline service to handle problems.
- A Christmas gift in July (they will remember it!).

Immediate recognition for new customers

Once a new customer signs on, smother him/her/them with attention. In business markets, introduce the new customer to the company president or other high official. In consumer markets, a 'welcome aboard' letter signed by a director can serve the same function.

Other welcome aboard activities may include the offering of a credit facility or credit card or some benefit selected from the customer benefits package.

Special benefits for special customers

When you have a good customer, reward them royally and give them special treatment. It doesn't have to cost much to have a high impact.

As a 'frequent flyer', I am upgraded by TWA from tourist class to business class automatically – provided there is an empty seat. The marginal extra cost is more than made up by my frequent flying on TWA.

Compare this with my treatment as a member of KLM's Flying Dutchman Club: I was turned away from the business class lounge at JFK airport when travelling tourist class with my family. No benefit, no fly . . .

'The Advisory Board' benefit can also be offered to special customers with excellent results. This idea was developed years ago by *Chemical Week* magazine. Each year the publisher wrote to thousands of long-term subscribers asking them to serve on the *Chemical Week* Advisory Board. An impressive certificate, suitable for framing, was provided to those who agreed (the majority).

A large percentage of the Advisory Board members cooperated with readership surveys, provided suggestions on an *ad hoc* basis to the Advisory Board Secretariat – and remained subscribers for the rest of their careers!

Benefits to get back 'lost' customers

Here is a key principle of customer marketing: never let a good customer get away from you – or stay away.

When you notice that a customer has left you, or is dropping away, take action. Ask if there is a problem. If so, fix the problem if at all possible. If you can't fix the problem, explain why and offer some kind of compensation.

The cost of getting a good customer back is generally only a fraction of the cost of creating a good customer.

And a dissatisfied ex-customer can do you damage that you'll never even know about! So phone them, send them a letter, pay a visit – do anything to prevent a good customer from slipping away.

Innovative retailer Murray Raphel sends his inactive customers a cheque or coupon worth $10. The reactivated customers usually spend many times the value of the credit. More important, they come back in the store, and tend to keep coming back.

Benefits to upgrade customers

It's nice to have steady customers. But it's even nicer to have steady customers who buy more!

Thus you must offer benefits to move your customers up the customer pyramid. It simply won't happen unless you stimulate the process with techniques such as:

- offering special terms if the customer extends his contract for a longer term;
- stimulating purchases with 'free gifts', premiums, discounts;
- stimulating additional purchases of an item on special terms;
- cross-selling: offering an item or service which complements something the customer already purchased;
- and anything else you can think of to stimulate more purchases and satisfaction.

You may also want to consider financial rewards: frequent buyer discounts, volume discounts, saving stamp plans and other techniques are often used to upgrade good customers and reward their loyalty.

Customer benefits package – the InterWidget case

Bill de Vries sat down with his marketing and sales staff and developed a number of benefits for InterWidget customers, prospects and suspects.

InterWidget benefits to identify customers

InterWidget had two customer identification programmes. For Suspects, it offered a *free booklet* on 'How to Improve Machine Tool Manufacturing', written by a recognised guru on the subject. This concept was expanded with free, half-day *seminars* on the same subject with the guru as the featured speaker.

People who requested the booklet or attended the seminar were screened, qualified and rated as to their status as prospects.

InterWidget benefits to create customers

Once it knew its prospects, InterWidget offered a variety of benefits to induce them to become customers. But these benefits were tailored to the type of customer to be created:

- A *one-year free service offer* was made to Topper customer candidates.
- A *three-month free trial* of InterWidget products was offered to Good Guy candidates.
- A *free demonstration* and presentation of Widget products was offered to Low Boy candidates.

InterWidget benefits to maintain customers

- InterWidget extended its highly successful customer satisfaction survey as an ongoing customer satisfaction programme consisting of follow-up calls to customers within one week after a shipment was delivered or service repair was made. The customers were asked if their shipment had arrived and was as ordered. The service customers were asked if the problem was resolved. If there was any dissatisfaction, immediate action was taken and the customer was notified. In all cases, the customers received a relevant 'personal' letter from Bill de Vries.
- A Widget Users Group (WUG) was also established for all customers. WUG had quarterly meetings combining seminars plus social entertainment and an informative newsletter. The WUG kept InterWidget in touch with its customers, and provided a forum for exchanging ideas.
- Topper customers were invited to join 'The Inner Circle' of WUG which featured a yearly 'study trip' to visit machine tool manufacturers in exotic, far-off places. These proved to be very popular. And while the cost was high, so was the pay-off!

InterWidget benefits to upgrade customers

- To upgrade Good customers to Topper status, InterWidget held out the promise of joining 'The Inner Circle' – the yearly study trip.
- Low Boy customers were enticed to move up to Good status as the yearly service contract fee was waived on some products.

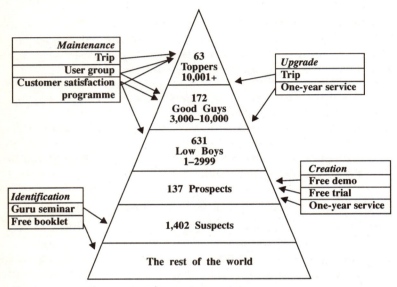

Figure 24 *InterWidget customer benefits*

Step 6

Select Methods and Media

As discussed in Part 1 of this book, virtually every marketing and sales medium and method can be used for customer marketing. The trick is to select methods and media which will:

- succeed in reaching the goal of identifying, creating, maintaining and upgrading customers;
- do the job for the least cost.

There are no hard and fast rules about which medium to apply when and where. But it is obvious that the most personal, most effective – and most expensive – media and methods may be required to achieve the toughest assignments: *creating* and *upgrading* customers.

Which media and methods are best for you? You may wish to analyse your own situation by reviewing the descriptions of the

Personal media	Identify	Create	Maintain	Upgrade
• External sales force	☐	☐	☐	☐
• Internal sales force	☐	☐	☐	☐
• Support/Service staff	☐	☐	☐	☐
• Business mail and calls	☐	☐	☐	☐
• Business events (shows, seminars)	☐	☐	☐	☐
Semi-personal media				
• Telemarketing	☐	☐	☐	☐
• Direct mail	☐	☐	☐	☐
Non-personal media				
• Response advertising	☐	☐	☐	☐
• Radio and TV commercials	☐	☐	☐	☐
• Publicity	☐	☐	☐	☐
• Yellow Pages	☐	☐	☐	☐
• POS, coupons, etc	☐	☐	☐	☐

Figure 25 *Methods and media checklist*

key customer marketing media and methods below. Then tick off which you are using – or should be using – to identify, acquire, maintain and upgrade your customers.

Personal media and methods

- *External sales force*
  No medium is so effective in making, keeping and upgrading customers as a salesperson who is able to listen to the prospect, identify his problem and translate the salesperson's product into a solution. But there is also no more expensive medium: the cost per sales call is over £75 in many countries – and rising.
- *Internal sales force*
  Less expensive, of course, than the external sales force, and normally very cost-effective when handling existing customers. Less useful for converting prospects to first-time buyers unless the product or service has a low price or other barrier.
- *Support/Service staff*
  Many companies are discovering that their support, service and maintenance people can become a secret weapon in the competitive battle for customers and sales. Why? Because these people are often able to enter a customer's premises, talk with the users and decision makers in a non-threatening, non-sales situation, and find out what the customer's needs and problems are. The customer may be hesitant to discuss his equipment problems with the salesman with an order form in his blue suit. But the bespectacled service fellow in jeans is no threat. Success in using support and service staff as marketing media comes when you train them to spot business opportunities, give them the tools (such as structured visit report forms) and, above all, give them the incentives (both monetary and praise) for a job well done.
- *Business mail*
  Business mail is a sales visit substitute. Instead of visiting the customer or prospect, the salesperson writes a 'personal' note. For example, the people who rent out copying machines produce from their customer database 'personal letters' for their salespeople to sign which read something like this:

Dear Joe

Just a short note to let you know that I heard around the office that the monthly rental price of the WIDGETS may go up by 5 per cent next year. Now, I think that I can get my boss to keep the price for you the same as this year if you can commit now. Just put your signature on the enclosed extension request, and I'll take care of everything. Please phone if you have any questions.

Best regards,

Sam Salesperson

And after signing the computer-produced letter, the salesperson then writes a personal note in his or her own handwriting:

PS Give my regards to Mary.

Such 'personal' letters are sent out by the hundreds – or thousands, in some cases.

- *Business phone calls*
  Business phone calls work like business mail, but instead of a letter use a semi-programmed telephone script which the salesperson can adapt for each customer he or she phones.
- *Business events (shows, exhibitions, seminars, etc)*
  Business events are useful for identifying potential customers and for maintaining the relationship with current customers. They can be cost–effective since salesperson time can be leveraged in a 'one-on-many' group situation instead of the normal 'one-to-one' sales situation.

Semi-personal media

- *Telemarketing*
  Telemarketing is the fastest growing customer marketing medium. Although cost per contact is higher than for direct mail, it is not unusual to make effective contact with 50 to 80 per cent or more designated persons in a market segment. Telemarketing can also be powerful and persuasive, if handled properly. (If poorly done, telemarketing can kill

your reputation!) Telemarketing is also quite flexible. After only 50 to 100 calls, you know whether or not your list, offer and script need adjustment.

- *Direct mail*
  Direct mail has many advantages for customer marketing. It is highly targeted: you can send it to very specific groups and segments. It is also reasonably personal since it is addressed to one individual, and 'signed' by another. And most people perceive a letter as the most personal form of written communication between human beings. Primary disadvantages: mailing costs are rising and sure to go higher – but response rates remain the same or are falling. Direct mail is also a bit inflexible: there is a lead time of a month or two to get a major mailing sent, and you don't know your success until a week or a month after the mailing date.

Non-personal media

- *Response advertising*
  This can be highly cost-effective for identifying prospects and even generating sales for lower-priced articles. Cost per contact is generally low, normally below 5p per subscriber.
- *Radio and TV commercials*
  Response from radio commercials may work – but usually not as effectively as TV commercials, where a product/service can be demonstrated and the response address and/or telephone number can be shown. Response TV is becoming more popular with the development of highly segmented cable services: the cost goes down while the chance of reaching a particular segment goes up.
- *Publicity*
  Publicity and free press play can be a highly effective and cheap customer marketing medium. (Just make sure you get your address or telephone number in the article!)
- *Yellow Pages*
  Sometimes excellent for having potential customers identify themselves to you. (By mistake, my company name is listed – in very small type face like this – in the Yellow Pages under 'Home computers'. And yet I get at least one call a week asking for Commodore 64 software!)

- *Point-of-sale, coupons, on-pack/in-pack folders, etc*
  In fact, just about any medium – including bookmatches – can be used for customer marketing. As long as it has a realistic chance of contributing to the customer marketing objectives of identifying, creating, keeping and developing customers.

Methods and media – the InterWidget case

Bill de Vries found that while talking about the benefits package with his marketing and sales staff, the discussion quickly turned to how these benefits would be communicated. And so they stayed an extra hour and came up with these choices of methods and media.

InterWidget methods and media to identify customers

- *Response advertisements* in trade publications offering the free booklet were targeted at suspects.
- *Direct mail* offering the guru seminar was sent to prospect and suspect decision makers.
- *Telemarketing* was used to qualify leads and follow up non-response.

InterWidget methods and media to create customers

- The *external sales force* was the only logical way for InterWidget to acquire new business.

InterWidget methods and media to maintain customers

- Regular sales and service contacts via the *internal sales force* were the primary customer maintenance media, supplemented by:
- *Courtesy visits* by the external sales force to Topper customers; and
- *Business calls* and *business mail* to both Topper and Good customers.

InterWidget methods and media to upgrade customers

- The *external sales force* was focused on upgrading Good customers.

- The *internal sales force* had the task of upgrading Low Boy customers.

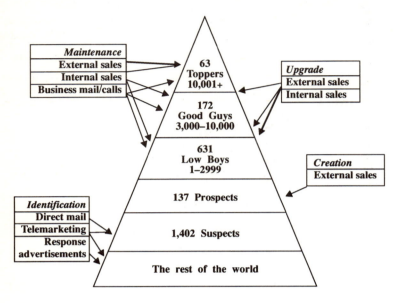

Figure 26 *InterWidget methods and media*

Customer marketing budget

Bill de Vries and his staff made detailed budgets and plans for implementing the customer benefits package and the selling methods and media. A summary of their efforts is illustrated. (Details can be found in the InterWidget spreadsheets.)

Notice that the InterWidget customer marketing budget allocates funds three ways:

- by customer goals (identification, creation, maintenance and upgrading);
- per type of method/media (customer benefits, sales force and semi/non–personal);
- per customer (suspects/prospects, Low Boys, Goods and Toppers).

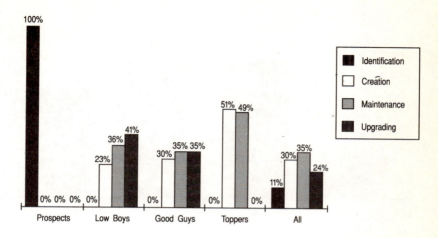

Figure 27 *Customer marketing budget: per customer goal*

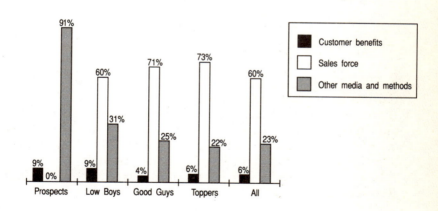

Figure 28 *Customer marketing budget: per methods and media*

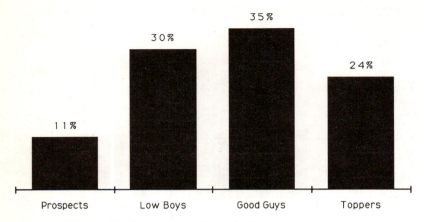

Figure 29 *Customer marketing budget: per customer type*

Step 7
Get Customer Orientated

Customer marketing simply won't work unless you and everyone else in your company have a strong customer orientation. What is a customer orientation?

Well, you have it when you know who your customers are . . . you know what they want and expect from you . . . you know what they think about you . . . you are always seeking more customers . . . you are determined never to lose a customer . . . you realise that, without customers, you might as well shut the door and go home.

A customer orientation doesn't evolve automatically. It must be actively introduced into an organisation, nurtured and maintained until it becomes an integral part of the company culture. Even then, constant monitoring is necessary to ensure that customer orientation sticks.

Customer orientation – the InterWidget case

Here are the programmes and activities which Bill de Vries used to introduce a customer orientation at InterWidget:

Phone a customer a day programme
Bill has an arrangement with his secretary to phone one customer a day. And when he gets the customer on the phone he says: 'Good morning, Mr Customer. I'm Bill de Vries of InterWidget, and I'm phoning for two reasons. First, I want you to know how much we appreciate your business. We're really proud to count you among our customers.'

Bill can almost hear the customer think: 'What's going on here? This is the first time anybody from InterWidget has phoned without trying to sell me something! What's going to happen next?' Bill then continues with: 'The second point, Mr Customer, is that I'd like your advice, ideas and opinions on how we can do a better job for you.'

And the customer thinks: 'Gosh, these people from InterWidget are OK. Because they are asking the smartest man in the world for advice – me!'

More often than not, Bill then hears things like: 'Did you know that it sometimes takes more than a minute before someone answers your phone.' Or 'I think your service department is excellent – they need a bit more recognition.' Or 'We'd like to do more business with you, but only if we get a credit account. Can we talk about it?' Or 'I've got no problem with InterWidget – in fact, now that you're on the phone, I'd like to discuss a new order.'

Key account contact by management
InterWidget's key accounts represented their profitable business. Bill makes sure that he and his other managers have personal contact with key accounts at least once a month.

Rewards for 'customer results'
Salespeople are generally rewarded for sales volume. Bill de Vries added rewards for customer results as well at InterWidget: X points for gaining a new customer, minus X points for losing a customer. Implementing customer scores – among the sales force and sales management – worked wonders for InterWidget.

Service staff incentives to develop customers
InterWidget's service and support staff have intensive customer contact. Thus they are in a position to identify customer needs and new business opportunities. So Bill offered them incentives, both tangible (bonus, trips, etc) and intangible (awards and recognition). But incentives were not enough. His service and support staff also needed training or other tools such as a 'Business Opportunities Report Form' to be filled in after each visit to a customer site.

Training for the 'front-line troops' . . .
At InterWidget, as at most companies, telephonists, receptionists, secretaries and the accounts staff have frequent customer contact. As such, they are the front-line troops of customer marketing. Thus the way they deal with customers and prospects determines to a large extent attitudes towards your organisation. Bill scheduled telephone skills training programmes for his front-line troops. But he also found it doesn't hurt to check out the troops once in a while. He phones his switchboard regularly to see how callers are handled, and reviews the methods his credit controllers use to 'encourage' customers to pay overdue invoices.

Customer orientation programmes for everybody

Last, but certainly not least, Bill de Vries made sure that every employee was aware of the company's customer goals – and how far along they all were in meeting them. He also announced the results of market research reports on how InterWidget's customers – and non-customers – rated the company and the competition.

Bill even had some video tapes made of some happy – and not so happy – customers. He had these shown to all staff – including the workers on the factory floor. For some of them, it was the first time they had ever laid eyes on an InterWidget customer! The improvement in higher quality was immediately measurable.

Record Customer Behaviour

Customer marketing requires you to record customer behaviour such as:

- RFM indicators per customer
- products purchased
- media methods creating transactions
- returns
- payment history.

With this information you can learn how to fine-tune your customer marketing activities, to make more customers, more profits and incur lower costs.

But how can you record customer behaviour if you have thousands of customers? Some businesses which rely on computer-based order processing systems have no major problem, ie banks, credit card companies, mail order, publications, etc.

Retailers who want to use customer marketing usually have to introduce some kind of credit or customer card which brings together information about the customer and products purchased at the cash register.

Fast-moving consumer goods companies are experimenting with bonus stamp systems and 'club'-type activities.

It is not always easy to record customer data in the consumer marketplace. But the use of universal product codes plus data-capturing hardware such as optical readers and light pens are making the process easier.

Recording customer behaviour – the InterWidget case

InterWidget spent considerable time and effort keeping track of customer behaviour and registering that behaviour in their customer database. At the end of the year, Bill made up a new pyramid showing InterWidget's 'customer results'.

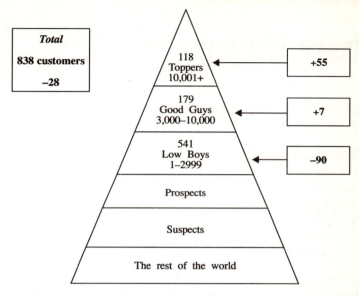

Figure 30 *InterWidget's customer pyramid after customer marketing*

And as Figure 31 shows, InterWidget's customer results pretty much matched the customer goals set at the beginning of the year.

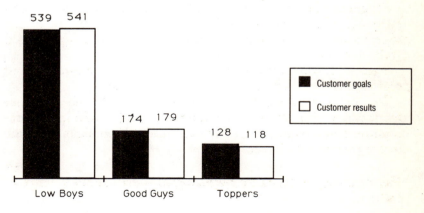

Figure 31 *Customer goals versus customer results*

Step 9

Analyse Results

Customer marketing is a learning process based on a continuing flow of customer and market information. And when this information is analysed, you learn some lessons. And then you apply the lessons learned to revisions in your marketing efforts.

The kinds of question you can answer from effective customer marketing include:

- Who are our clients?
- Who buys what?
- Which clients are profitable? Which are not?
- Who decides, buys and uses our products?
- Which distribution channel works best?
- Which customer benefits work best?
- Which media, methods and messages work best?
- What is the ROI on our marketing money?
- How should we allocate our marketing budget?

Analysing results – the InterWidget case

Bill de Vries was quite pleased about the bottom line impact of customer marketing on InterWidget's financial results: more than 100 per cent increase in profits despite:

- a 3 per cent increase in marketing and sales costs;
- a 10 per cent increase in overheads to set up and manage the customer database; and
- a 3 per cent decrease in the number of customers!

Here is how it looked on a chart:

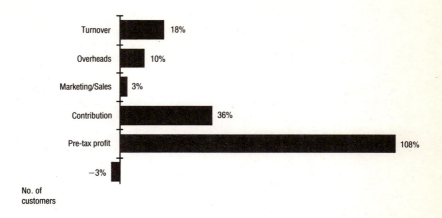

Figure 32 *Customer marketing: the profit pay-off for InterWidget*

But to really understand the impact of customer marketing on InterWidget, Bill went to the primary source of the good news – the InterWidget customers. He made this comparison of changes which occurred among each customer type:

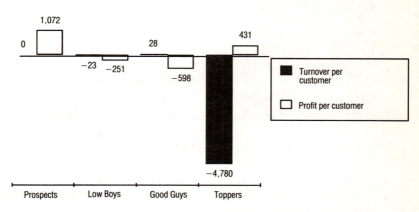

Figure 33 *Financial impact: per customer type*

Bill de Vries took a lot of time to look at the before/after analysis. He concluded that the real reasons for the customer marketing

85

profit pay-off were to be seen in two categories: Prospects and Toppers.

- *Prospects*. Bill noticed that marketing and sales costs per prospect decreased substantially. This was a direct result of selecting the right methods and media, ie replacing sales force prospecting efforts with semi- and non-personal media and methods.
- *Toppers*. Turnover per customer dropped 4,780. This apparent decrease in spending reflected the fact that new acquisitions and upgrades from the Low Boy and Good Guy categories joined Topper status during the year, thus diluting Topper turnover per customer performance for the entire period.

  But profit per Topper customer increased substantially, again owing to a better allocation of marketing and sales budget and effort.

As a result, overall results per customer were an increase in turnover and profit per customer of £906 and £293 respectively.

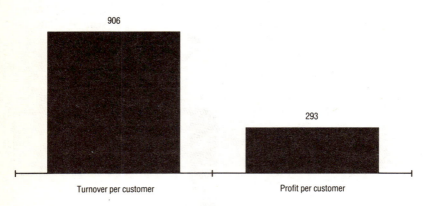

Figure 34 *Financial impact: all customers*

Bill's final conclusion was that InterWidget's profit pay-off from customer marketing would continue – or even increase – in the following year. He knew he could reduce sales and marketing costs even more because his primary task would be maintaining InterWidget's new Toppers, an activity which should cost less time and money than upgrading them.

And the newly upgraded and acquired customers, if maintained, would perform for the entire year, thus bringing up turnover and profits per customer category across the board.

Step 10

Revise Your Customer Programmes

When you have made your analysis, you should know what worked, what didn't and why. And in the future you can focus on what works:

- winning segments;
- winning products;
- winning benefits;
- winning media/methods.

The losers you dump without ceremony, and pledge to yourself never to make the same mistake twice.

But remember: today's winner is tomorrow's loser. The world around you, your competitors, the technology, your customers' needs and wants keep changing. So you have to keep on gathering customer marketing information, keep on analysing it, keep on testing.

Revising customer programmes – the InterWidget case

Bill de Vries was very satisfied with the results of customer marketing. The customer satisfaction programme was especially successful, identifying a lot of customer needs which had not been identified in the past. And since the response from customers led to personal discussions, a number of unexpected orders closed. It paid for itself.

But Bill and his staff also noted a number of activities and areas which could have been better. For instance:

- The Widget User Group took a lot of time and energy to organise – and sometimes the meetings turned into 'gripe sessions'. The activity will be streamlined.

- While the InterWidget marketing and sales managers got along personally, there was a good deal of confusion over who was responsible for which activity, especially telemarketing.
- The guru seminar was a disappointment. The man arrived late and delivered his speech in a routine manner. Fortunately, the audience was not very large. The programme was replaced by a one-day Widget Workshop using Widget technicians as trainers.
- Despite an investment of almost £60,000 in a customer database – and a person to manage it – the system was difficult for many salespeople to use, and it took too much time to get the information Bill wanted every month.

As Bill de Vries discovered, internal factors more often than not have a great impact on the success of your marketing and sales efforts. If some of the problems he encountered seem familiar, you may wish to subject your business to a customer marketing audit as explained in Part 3.

Customer Marketing Spreadsheets

The following pages contain the spreadsheets which Bill de Vries at InterWidget used to develop his customer marketing analyses and plans, and are referred to in the preceding pages. You may want to base your own spreadsheets on this model.

InterWidget financial results last year

Turnover	3,642,954
Cost of product	1,827,571
Gross margin	1,814,973
Marketing/Salespeople	601,950
Marketing/Sales: other	396,616
Total marketing/sales	998,566
Contribution	816,407
Overheads	596,297
Pre-tax profit	220,110
Number of customers	866
Turnover per customer	4,207
Pre-tax profit per customer	254

Financial analysis of InterWidget – last year's results

Financial analysis per customer type	Prospects	Low Boy customers	Good customers	Topper customers	Total
Number of prospects	137				137
Number of customers		631	172	63	866
Turnover	0	943,940	1,211,871	1,487,143	3,642,954
Total cost of product	0	486,487	605,638	735,446	1,827,571
Total/Gross margin	0	457,003	606,233	751,737	1,814,973
Marketing/Sales: salespeople	150,488	150,488	150,488	150,488	601,950
Marketing/Sales: other	99,154	99,154	99,154	99,154	396,616
Total marketing/sales	249,642	249,642	249,642	249,642	998,566
Contribution	− 249,642	207,361	356,592	502,096	816,407
Overheads	149,074	149,074	149,074	149,074	596,297
Pre-tax profit	− 398,716	58,287	207,517	353,021	220,110
Profit as % of sales	NA	6%	17%	24%	6%
Marketing/Sales ROI	− 160%	23%	83%	141%	22%
% customers	NA	73%	20%	7%	100%
% turnover	NA	26%	33%	41%	100%
% profit	NA	9%	34%	57%	100%

Financial analysis per customer type	Prospects	Low Boy customers	Good customers	Topper customers	Total
Turnover per customer	0	1,496	7,046	23,605	4,207
Margin per customer	0	724	3,525	11,932	2,096
Marketing and sales/costs per customer	1,822	396	1,451	3,963	1,153
Contribution per customer	− 1,822	329	1,206	5,660	580
Overheads per customer	1,088	236	867	2,366	689
Pre-tax profit per customer	− 2,910	92	1,206	5,604	254
Breakeven no. of customers	NA	551	113	33	761

InterWidget market analysis – customer base

Customer base description (actual)	Low Boy customers	Good customers	Topper customers	Total
>500 employees	3	27	12	42
250–500 employees	13	74	22	109
100–250 employees	183	42	19	244
1–100 employees	432	29	10	471
Total customers	631	172	63	866

Customer base description (%)	Low Boy customers	Good customers	Topper customers	All customers
>500 employees	7%	64%	29%	5%
250–500 employees	12%	68%	20%	13%
100–250 employees	75%	17%	8%	28%
1–100 employees	92%	6%	2%	54%
Total customers	73%	20%	7%	100%

InterWidget market analysis – Market description:
Machine tool industry

Market size (companies):

>500 employees	56	2%
250–500 employees	146	6%
100–250 employees	598	23%
1–100 employees	1,748	69%
Total market	2,548	100%

Non-customer distribution (actual)	*Prospect distribution*	*Suspect distribution*	*All non-customers*
>500 employees	4	10	14
250–500 employees	13	24	37
100–250 employees	73	281	354
1–100 employees	83	1,194	1,277
Total non-customers	173	1,509	1,682

Non-customer distribution (%)	*Prospect distribution*	*Suspect distribution*	*All non-customers*
>500 employees	2%	1%	1%
250–500 employees	8%	2%	2%
100–250 employees	42%	19%	21%
1–100 employees	48%	79%	76%
Total non-customers	10%	90%	100%

Customer share by type and total	*Low Boy customers*	*Good customers*	*Topper customers*	*Share per segment*
>500 employees	5%	48%	21%	75%
250–500 employees	9%	51%	15%	75%
100–250 employees	31%	7%	3%	41%
1–100 employees	25%	2%	1%	27%
Overall share	25%	7%	2%	34%

InterWidget customer goals

Customer goals next year	Prospects	Low Boy customers	Good customers	Topper customers	Total
Prospects (start)	137				137
Existing customers (start)		631	172	63	866
Expected fall-off	60	95	20	0	115
Existing customers (net)	NA	536	152	63	751
Identification goals	140				140
Creation goals	NA	70	15	5	90
Maintenance goals	NA	469	117	63	649
Upgrading goals					
Upgrade to Toppers	NA	25	35	0	60
Upgrade to Good	NA	42	0	0	42
Total upgrade out	NA	67	35	0	102
Total upgrade in	NA	0	42	60	102
Totals after plan period					
Prospects	217				217
Customers		539	174	128	841

Customer maintenance budget

Methods and media budget – maintenance	Prospects	Low Boy customers	Good customers	Topper customers	Total
Customer maintain goals	NA	469	117	63	649
Personal media					
• External sales force	0	20,000	40,000	80,000	140,000
• Internal sales force	0	20,000	30,000	10,000	60,000
Subtotal sales force	0	40,000	70,000	90,000	200,000
• Business mail/calls	0	5,000	3,000	2,000	10,000
• User group/trips/ seminar	0	5,000	3,000	5,000	13,000
Semi-personal media					
• Direct mail shots	0	0	0	0	0
• Newsletter	0	5,000	2,000	1,000	8,000
• Telemarketing/ outbound	0	0	0	0	0
• Customer service programme	0	50,000	40,000	20,000	110,000
Non-personal media					
• Coupon advertising	0	0	0	0	0
• Response radio/TV ads	0	0	0	0	0
• Publicity/PR	0	3,000	2,000	1,000	6,000
• Other	0	0	0	0	0
Subtotal other non-sales	0	68,000	50,000	29,000	147,000
Subtotal maintenance	0	108,000	120,000	119,000	347,000

Customer upgrading budget

Methods and media budget – upgrading	Prospects	Low Boy customers	Good customers	Topper customers	Total
Upgrade to Toppers	NA	25	35	0	60
Upgrade to Good	NA	42	0	0	42
Total upgrade out	NA	67	35	0	102
Total upgrade in	NA	0	42	60	102
Personal media					
● External sales force	0	80,000	95,000	0	175,000
● Internal sales force	0	25,000	20,000	0	45,000
Subtotal sales force	0	105,000	115,000	0	220,000
● Business mail/calls	0	2,000	1,000	0	3,000
● User group/trips/ seminar	0	5,000	3,000	0	8,000
Semi-personal media					
● Direct mail shots	0	2,000	0	0	2,000
● Newsletter	0	2,000	0	0	2,000
● Telemarketing/ outbound	0	7,000	1,000	0	8,000
● Customer service programme	0	0	0	0	0
Non-personal media					
● Coupon advertising	0	0	0	0	0
● Response radio/TV ads	0	0	0	0	0
● Publicity/PR	0	0	0	0	0
● Other	0	0	0	0	0
Subtotal other non–sales	0	18,000	5,000	0	23,000
Subtotal upgrading	0	123,000	120,000	0	243,000

Customer identification and creation budget

Methods and media budget – identify and create	Prospects	Low Boy customers	Good customers	Topper customers	Total
Prospecting goals	140				
Customer creation goals		70	15	5	90
Personal media					
● External sales force	0	10,000	25,000	50,000	85,000
● Internal sales force	0	25,000	35,000	35,000	95,000
Subtotal sales force	0	35,000	60,000	85,000	180,000
● Business mail/calls	0	0	0	0	0
● User group/trips/ seminar	10,000	0	5,000	7,000	22,000
Semi-personal media					
● Direct mail shots	35,000	15,000	15,000	10,000	75,000
● Newsletter	0	5,000	10,000	5,000	20,000
● Telemarketing/ outbound	18,000	10,000	10,000	10,000	48,000
● Customer service programme	0	0	0	0	0
Non-personal media					
● Coupon advertising	45,000	0	0	0	45,000
● Response radio/TV ads	0	0	0	0	0
● Publicity/PR	5,000	5,000	5,000	5,000	20,000
● Other	0	0	0	0	0
Subtotal other non–sales	113,000	35,000	45,000	37,000	230,000
Subtotal identification	113,000				113,000
Subtotal creation		70,000	105,000	122,000	297,000

Customer marketing budget
per customer type

Methods and media budget – customer type	Prospects	Low Boy customers	Good customers	Topper customers	Total
Number	140	539	174	128	841
Personal media					
• External sales force	0	110,000	160,000	130,000	400,000
• Internal sales force	0	70,000	85,000	45,000	200,000
Subtotal sales force	0	180,000	245,000	175,000	600,000
• Business mail/calls	0	7,000	4,000	2,000	13,000
• User group/trips/ seminar	10,000	10,000	11,000	12,000	43,000
Semi-personal media					
• Direct mail shots	35,000	17,000	15,000	10,000	77,000
• Newsletter	0	12,000	12,000	6,000	30,000
• Telemarketing/ outbound	18,000	17,000	11,000	10,000	56,000
• Customer service programme	0	50,000	40,000	20,000	110,000
Non-personal media					
• Coupon advertising	45,000	0	0	0	45,000
• Response radio/TV ads	0	0	0	0	0
• Publicity/PR	5,000	8,000	7,000	6,000	26,000
• Other	0	0	0	0	0
Subtotal other	113,000	121,000	100,000	66,000	400,000
Grand total	113,000	301,000	345,000	241,000	1,000,000
% marketing budget	11%	30%	35%	24%	100%
Cost per type	807	558	1,983	1,883	1,189

Customer marketing budget
per customer goal

Methods and media budget – customer goals	Identify prospects	Create customers	Maintain customers	Upgrade customers	Total
Prospect goals	140				
Customer goals		90	649	102	841
Personal media					
● External sales force	0	85,000	140,000	175,000	400,000
● Internal sales force	0	95,000	60,000	45,000	200,000
Subtotal sales force	0	180,000	200,000	220,000	600,000
● Business mail/calls	0	0	10,000	3,000	13,000
● User group/trips/ seminar	10,000	12,000	13,000	8,000	43,000
Semi-personal media					
● Direct mail shots	35,000	40,000	0	2,000	77,000
● Direct mail catalogues	0	20,000	8,000	2,000	30,000
● Telemarketing/ outbound	18,000	30,000	0	8,000	56,000
● Customer satisfaction	0	0	110,000	0	110,000
Non-personal media					
● Coupon advertising	45,000	0	0	0	45,000
● Response radio/TV ads	0	0	0	0	0
● Publicity/PR	5,000	15,000	6,000	0	26,000
● Other	0	0	0	0	0
Subtotal other	113,000	117,000	147,000	23,000	400,000
Grand total	113,000	297,000	347,000	243,000	1,000,000
% marketing budget	11%	30%	35%	24%	100%
Cost per prospect	807				807
Cost per customer		3,300	535	2,382	1,189

**Customer marketing budget –
summary**

Methods and media budget – summary	Suspects/ Prospects	Low Boy customers	Good customers	Topper customers	Total	% of budget
Customer identification						
Customer benefits, etc	10,000	0	0	0	0	0%
External/Internal sales	0	0	0	0	0	0%
Other media/methods	103,000	0	0	0	0	0%
Total identification	113,000	0	0	0	113,000	11%
Customer creation						
Customer benefits, etc	0	10,000	5,000	7,000	22,000	2%
External/Internal sales	0	35,000	60,000	85,000	180,000	18%
Other media/methods	0	25,000	40,000	30,000	95,000	10%
Total creation	0	70,000	105,000	122,000	297,000	30%
Customer maintenance						
Customer benefits, etc	0	10,000	6,000	7,000	23,000	2%
External/Internal sales	0	40,000	70,000	90,000	200,000	20%
Other media/methods	0	58,000	44,000	22,000	124,000	12%
Total maintenance	0	108,000	120,000	119,000	347,000	35%
Customer upgrading						
Customer benefits, etc	0	7,000	4,000	0	11,000	1%
External/Internal sales	0	105,000	115,000	0	220,000	22%
Other media/methods	0	11,000	1,000	0	12,000	1%
Total upgrading	0	123,000	120,000	0	243,000	24%
Budget Totals						
Customer benefits, etc	10,000	27,000	15,000	14,000	56,000	6%
External/Internal sales	0	180,000	245,000	175,000	600,000	60%
Other media/methods	103,000	94,000	85,000	52,000	231,000	23%
Total budget	113,000	301,000	345,000	241,000	1,000,000	100%
% marketing budget	11%	30%	35%	24%	100%	

InterWidget Customer Results

	Prospects	Low Boy customers	Good customers	Topper customers	Total
Existing customers (start)	137	631	172	63	866
Actual fall-off	NA	88	23	3	114
Existing customers (end)	NA	543	149	60	752
Identification results	100				100
Creation results	−87	66	14	6	86
Maintenance results	NA	475	119	60	654
Upgrading results					
Upgraded to Toppers	NA	22	30	0	52
Upgraded to Good	NA	46	0		46
Total upgrade out	NA	68	30	0	98
Total upgrade in	NA	0	46	52	98
Customer results					
Prospects	151				
Customers		541	179	118	838
Customer plan					
Prospects	217				
Customers		539	174	128	841
Plan versus results					
Prospects	−66				
Customers		2	5	−10	−3
Change in percentage turnover and customers					
% turnover	NA	−7%	−4%	11%	NA
% customers	NA	−39%	12%	27%	NA

Financial analysis of InterWidget – after customer marketing

Financial analysis per customer type	Prospects	Low Boy customers	Good customers	Topper customers	Total
Number of prospects	151				
Number of customers		541	179	118	838
Turnover fall-off customer	NA	58,351	82,858	36,902	178,110
Turnover maintain customer	NA	647,289	857,395	1,476,060	2,980,744
Turnover upgrade out	NA	46,138	108,075	0	154,213
Turnover upgrade in	NA	0	165,715	639,626	805,341
Turnover new customer	NA	45,057	52,233	68,806	166,096
Total turnover	0	796,835	1,266,276	2,221,394	4.284,504
Costs of product actual	0	410,868	632,827	1,098,530	2,142,225
Gross margin	0	385,967	633,449	1,122,864	2,142,280
Marketing/Sales: salespeople	0	187,215	246,537	179,542	613,294
Marketing/Sales: other	113,000	121,115	114,325	67,542	415,982
Marketing/Sales: costs	113,000	308,330	360,862	247,084	1,029,276
Contribution	−113,000	77,637	272,587	875,780	1,113,004
Overheads	163,670	163,670	163,670	163,670	654,679
Pre-tax profit	−276,670	−86,033	108,917	712,110	458,325
Profit as % of sales	NA	−11%	9%	32%	11%
Marketing/Sales ROI	NA	−28%	30%	288%	45%
% Turnover	NA	19%	30%	52%	100%
% Customers	NA	65%	21%	14%	100%
% Profit	NA	−12%	15%	97%	100%

Financial analysis per customer type	Prospects	Low Boy customers	Good customers	Topper customers	Total
Turnover per customer	0	1,473	7,074	18,825	5,113
Margin per customer	0	713	3,539	9,516	2,556
Marketing and sales/ costs per customer	751	209	1,723	3,058	295
Contribution per customer	−751	144	1,523	7,422	1,328
Overheads per customer	1,088	303	914	1,387	781
Pre-tax profit per customer	−1,838	−159	608	6,035	547
Breakeven no. of customers	NA	662	148	43	659

Before and after comparison of results at customer level

Differences after customer marketing	Prospects	Low Boy customers	Good customers	Topper customers	Total
Number of prospects	14				
Number of customers		−90	7	55	−28
Turnover per customer	0	−23	28	−4,780	906
Margin per customer	0	−11	14	−2,417	461
Marketing and sales costs per customer	−1,071	−187	271	−904	−858
Contribution per customer	1,071	−185	317	1,762	748
Overheads per customer	−1	66	48	−979	93
Pre-tax profit per customer	1,072	−251	−598	431	293
Breakeven no. of customers	NA	111	35	10	−102
Profit as % of sales	NA	−17%	−9%	−8%	5%
Marketing/Sales ROI	NA	−51%	−53%	147%	22%

Before and after comparison of results at company level

Before versus after customer marketing	Before CM	After CM	Difference amount	Difference %
Number of customers	866	838	−28	−3%
Turnover	3,642,954	4,284,504	641,550	18%
Cost of product actual	1,827,571	2,142,225	314,654	17%
Gross margin	1,814,973	2,142,280	327,307	18%
Marketing/Sales: salespeople	601,950	613,294	11,344	2%
Marketing/Sales: other	396,616	415,982	19,366	5%
Total marketing/sales	998,566	1,029,276	30,710	3%
Contribution	816,407	1,113,004	296,597	36%
Overheads	596,297	654,679	58,382	10%
Pre-tax profit	220,110	458,325	238,215	108%
Breakeven no. of customers	761	659	−102	−13%
Profit as % of sales	6%	11%	5%	77%
ROI on marketing/sales	22%	45%	22%	102%

Part 3:

Your Customer Marketing Audit

Many executives have asked me this question:

If customer marketing can deliver such a profit increase, why doesn't every company use it?

And my answer is this:

The customer marketing strategy is quite simple. But implementing the strategy is not.

More often than not, managers underestimate the internal changes in the minds of the people and the information systems which customer marketing requires.

Have you ever been in a company when the financial administration switched over to a new computer system? Chances are that the organisation was in chaos for six months or more, despite the fact that:

- the information (financial data) was highly structured; and
- the people involved (administrators) had relatively structured ways of thinking.

In a certain sense, customer marketing means switching over to a new computer system for the marketing and sales process. And the problems are greater than those involved with a financial system because:

- the information (customer data) is not always highly structured; and
- the people involved (marketing and sales) are not always highly structured in their way of thinking and acting.

How do you know if your company is ready for customer marketing?

In our experience of working with all kinds of companies, we have come to the conclusion that there are six organisational and informational factors which are critical to the success of your customer marketing activities:

Organisational factors

1. Your customer marketing management
2. Your customer marketing staff
3. Your customer marketing logistics

Informational factors

4. Your customer marketing information
5. Your customer marketing system
6. Your customer marketing communications

To make customer marketing work for you, you have to juggle with these six factors, paying attention first to one, then to the other to avoid letting one of them fall.

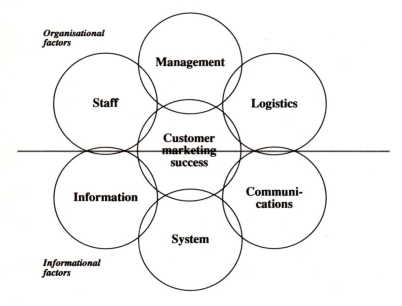

Figure 35 *Customer marketing critical success factors*

Is your company ready for customer marketing? You can learn more about these six critical success factors – and make a 'first cut' estimate of your degree of readiness – by completing this customer marketing audit.

It may take some time, and more information than you have in hand at the moment. But there is no better time to start than . . . *now*!

Customer marketing organisational factors

Customer marketing doesn't exist in a vacuum. It requires the involvement of virtually all departments in the company who must work together according to established procedures.

Now here is the organisational structure of the traditional marketing organisation, the typical line and staff 'tree' we are all familiar with.

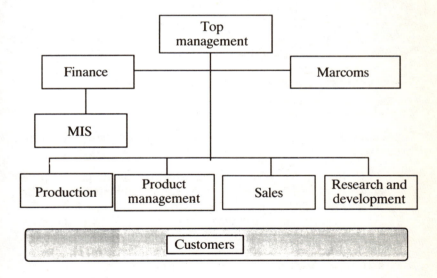

Figure 36 *Traditional marketing organisation*

Marcoms = Marketing communications
MIS = Management information systems

The organisational chart of a customer marketing organisation will probably look quite similar. After all, people have to know who their boss is. And they generally feel more comfortable working in an identifiable group.

But the way that different groups deal with customers – and each other – in a customer marketing organisation is quite different.

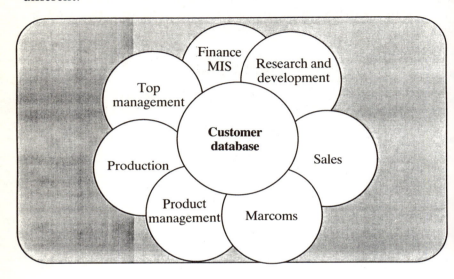

Figure 37 *Customer marketing organisation*

Marcoms = Marketing communications
MIS = Management information systems

The customer marketing organisation distinguishes itself in three ways:

1. The organisation sees itself existing surrounded by a sea of customers and prospects. Thus the organisation, and the people in it, live and breathe customers – all day long.
2. All working units are very much plugged into the customer database. Because that's where the information is which is critical to the task of the whole organisation: identifying, creating, maintaining and developing customers.
3. The working units are very much plugged into each other. Customer marketing doesn't allow time for solo-flying.

Teamwork and close coordination of tightly planned activities are required, and detailed working procedures must be worked out and followed closely.

There are two traditional areas of friction which a customer marketing organisation must solve:

- *Sales versus marketing.* It's an old story. Sales say marketing delivers lousy and poor campaigns. Marketing says sales doesn't follow up properly. Solution: give both groups customer objectives to achieve for which both are equally responsible.
- *Marketing versus EDP.* Most computer systems in companies were originally set up by the financial people – the bean counters – to keep track of accounts, send out invoices, handle the payroll. Thus the systems themselves – and the people who operate them – may not have much affinity with or interest in the marketing process, making cooperation sometimes difficult.

Now is the time to look at the organisational factors in your organisation: management, staff and logistics.

Critical Success Factor 1

Your Customer Marketing Management

Implementing (and maintaining) a customer marketing orientation in a company is not always easy. It can also require a substantial financial investment in systems, new people, training, etc. And also a lot of management time to manage the change which customer marketing brings to an organisation.

Thus customer marketing is unlikely to take hold or grow without strong management commitment to the philosophy, the activity, the process. And not just top management, but among line and staff managers throughout the organisation, because customer marketing can – and should – infiltrate every department of a company.

How do you rate your management commitment to customer marketing? Check it out! Put the appropriate score in the box.

+   = Good
0   = So-so
−   = Poor
?   = You don't know at this moment
NA = The item is not applicable to your organisation

Do your (top) managers:

Strategy
☐ plan the achievement of customer goals as well as financial goals?
☐ monitor customer results and take action where necessary?

Information
☐ base decisions on actual customer/prospect data?
☐ track customer satisfaction?

Budget
☐ allocate funds for customer marketing systems?

☐ allocate funds for customer orientation training?

☐ allocate time for making the organisation customer orientated?

☐ realise that creating customers requires an investment of time and money – but that the investment is the best your company will ever make?

Customer orientation

☐ phone or meet customers regularly?

☐ know if a key account is in trouble?

☐ reward sales staff on customer results as well as sales or margins?

☐ prefer to lose an order than lose a customer?

☐ ＿＿＿＿＿＿＿＿＿＿＿＿＿＿＿＿

☐ ＿＿＿＿＿＿＿＿＿＿＿＿＿＿＿＿

☐ ＿＿＿＿＿＿＿＿＿＿＿＿＿＿＿＿

☐ ＿＿＿＿＿＿＿＿＿＿＿＿＿＿＿＿

Critical Success Factor 2

Your Customer Marketing Staff

Customer marketing just won't work unless the company staff has the relevant know-how and experience, team spirit and a high degree of customer orientation.

Know-how and experience

You need a team of internal and external people with some know-how and experience in customer marketing to avoid reinventing the wheel and a costly learning curve.

Team spirit

Teamwork is also critical. Customer marketing doesn't exist in a vacuum. It requires the involvement of virtually all departments in the company who must work together according to established procedures.

Customer orientation

Customer marketing is not just a collection of methods, techniques and technologies. Customer marketing is an attitude, a way of doing business, a mentality.

You can have the most sophisticated customer marketing programme in the world – but it will fail if the customer's experience with your company doesn't reflect it.

For instance, a bank can send a lovely personal letter to current account customers suggesting they open a savings account, signed by the local bank manager. But when the customer enters the bank and is greeted by an uncaring teller who does not know – or care – about the campaign, the customer may walk out.

Customer marketing won't work until everyone shares the mentality which is reflected in a way of thinking along these lines:

'Our company – and my job – exists because we have customers.'
'We are in business to identify, make, keep and upgrade customers.'
'Losing a customer is bad news. Not getting him back is a tragedy.'
'Computer technology can help us to manage our relationships with our customers.'
'We should spend less time arguing with other departments and more time talking with our customers.'
'We will make mistakes, but a customer will forgive us if we apologise, fix the problem – and don't let it happen twice!'

How do you rate your customer marketing staff? Check it out!

+ = Good
0 = So-so
– = Poor
? = You don't know at this moment
NA = The item is not applicable to your organisation

Know-how and experience

☐ Customer marketing strategies and tactics.
Have you or your staff ever developed a customer marketing plan instead of a business plan? Allocated methods and media to reach specific customer objectives? Can you set up and operate a customer marketing programme for the sales force? And manage the overall process?

☐ Customer marketing mathematics.
Do you or your staff know how to forecast and calculate results using spreadsheets? Can they calculate marketing and sales ROI? Break-evens? Customer value? Customer lifetime?

☐ Direct marketing project management.
Many customer marketing activities and campaigns are

115

actually direct marketing projects which require a combination of inventiveness, creativity, entrepreneurship – and the ability to make sure that a thousand and one critical detailed steps are executed faultlessly. (Just one weak link in the chain of events, such as ordering the wrong list or a misprint on an envelope, can lose months of time and thousands of pounds.)

☐ Response-orientated marketing communications (internal).
Can you or your staff brief your agency on a direct mail package or response advertisement? Can you evaluate their output? Have you worked with telemarketing agencies? Have you set up or operated an in-house telemarketing effort?

☐ Response-orientated marketing communications (agency?).
Is your advertising agency committed to getting highly qualified response from direct mail and response advertising? Or are they more interested in making nice pictures, developing catchy headlines and winning prizes?

☐ Customer marketing systems.
Does your MIS department have experience in developing customer/prospect database systems? If not, do they have access to outside expertise and know-how?

Team spirit

☐ Sales.
Are your sales people really plugged into a customer marketing system? Do they cooperate with marketing people to improve the quality of marketing activities, lead generation programmes, etc?

☐ Marketing (communications).
Are your marketing people mature enough to realise that customer marketing is not the sole prerogative of their group – but a process that requires effort, dedication and involvement from other corporate units?

☐ Product management.
Do your product managers support customer marketing, or are they more obsessed with sales of (their) products?

☐ Finance/administration.
Do the 'bean counters' help you to keep customer scores in addition to counting pounds and pence?

☐ MIS.

Do the computer people have a special unit set up to handle (customer) marketing problems and programmes? Or are requests from marketing put on the bottom of the low priority pile?

☐ R&D.

Are your R&D people plugged into customer research and other information from the customer marketing systems which can guide their development efforts? Do they go out and meet customers?

☐ Production.

Are production people concerned about customer satisfaction, about high quality? Do they ever see customer satisfaction reports? Do they go out and meet happy – and unhappy – customers?

Customer orientation

How do you rate the customer orientation of these employee groups?

☐ Secretaries, receptionists, telephone staff
☐ Sales force
☐ Service staff
☐ Administration/Accounts staff
☐ Marketing executives
☐ Production crew
☐ Computing staff
☐ _____
☐ _____
☐ _____
☐ _____

Your Customer Marketing Logistics

All too often, the best-laid marketing and sales campaigns fail because of a breakdown in marketing and sales logistics, the nuts-and-bolts details of follow-up such as despatching samples or answering requests for documentation.

But the details of marketing and sales logistics often involve direct contact with customers and prospects. Thus sloppy organisation and lack of customer orientation in this area can be very costly in terms of lost customers and prospects who decide your company doesn't really want business.

How do you rate your customer marketing logistics? Check it out!

```
+   = Good
0   = So-so
–   = Poor
?   = You don't know at this moment
NA  = The item is not applicable to your organisation
```

☐ Database management.
Is all essential data on prospects, customers, dealers, sales force, marketing activities and products entered into the database? Is there a programme for maintaining the integrity of the data, and ensuring that changes are registered? Is security tight enough?

☐ Registration of transactions and response.
Is every customer/prospect contact registered in the database? All products or services purchased? Source code of media or marketing activity which influenced the sale?

☐ Follow-up of sales leads.
Are leads and requests for information being handled quickly and efficiently? (Try it out yourself sometime!)

☐ Order handling.
Is ordered merchandise being despatched swiftly? Services provided in time?

☐ Enquiry follow-up.
   If someone requests information, a quotation, etc, will he get it within three days? And if the information will take more time to prepare, are there procedures for sending him a note or ringing him up? And what about a telephone follow-up five days after despatch to ensure that the materials arrived, and to see if you can be of more service?

☐ Invoicing.
   Millions in cash flow are lost because companies can't get their statements and invoices out in time. How about your system?

☐ Complaint handling.
   Do you have built-in routines for handling – and solving – complaints?

☐ Returns.
   Do you handle returned merchandise effectively – not only the crediting procedures, but the inspection, restoration and handling of the goods?

☐ Chasing payment.
   Does your system generate polite – but firm – reminders on overdue bills? Do you have procedures to phone the customer and discuss the problem before sending irrevocable threats of court action?

Customer marketing informational factors

Customer marketing thrives on relevant, complete and up-to-date information on your customers and prospects. This is information which you can access easily, analyse and use as the basis of personalised communications.

What is the status of your information, your system to manage it and your communications?

Critical Success Factor 4

Your Customer Marketing Information

Customer marketing can only work when you have complete and relevant information on your customers and prospects and your relationship with them. Probably you have more information than you think, but it is dispersed throughout the organisation in computers, paper files, card files and shoe boxes.

What state is your customer marketing information in? Check it out!

+ = Good
0 = So-so
− = Poor
? = You don't know at this moment
NA = The item is not applicable to your organisation

Suggestion. Make a note in the space provided by each item where the information is currently stored in your organisation.

Prospect information (leads)

☐ Complete information. _____
Do you register key information on your prospects: name, address, age, sex, (consumer prospect) function, company name, type of business, size (business-to-business prospect) and any other characteristics which can help you to convert the prospect to customer status?

☐ Competitive products/services. _____
Do you know what products and services your prospects buy from your competitors?

☐ Qualification. _____
Have you a way to assign a score of the probability that the prospect will become a customer?

☐ Source code. _____
Do you know which marketing or sales activity generated each prospect?

☐ History of relationship. _____
Can you easily trace the flow of (interactive) communications between you and the prospect so that you can refer to these in future contacts, or in assessing the value of the prospect?

☐ Conversion to customer. _____
Do you have a way to signal when, and especially the reason why, a prospect becomes a customer? Or why you lose the sale and he becomes a customer of your competitor?

Customer information

☐ Complete information. _____
Do you register key information on your prospects: name, address, age, sex, (consumer prospect) function, company name, type of business, size (business-to-business prospect) and any other characteristics which can help you to convert the prospect to customer status?

☐ Products purchased. _____
Do you keep an accurate record of what products and services your customers buy from you?

☐ Competitive products/services. _____
Do you know what products and services your customers buy from your competitors?

☐ Credit behaviour. _____
Do you track the payment and credit behaviour of your customers?

☐ Source code. _____
Do you know which marketing or sales activity generated each customer?

☐ Reason for buying. _____
Are you able to capture and store the factors which made your customer buy from you in the first place – and keep on buying?

☐ History of relationship. _____
Can you easily trace the flow of (interactive) communications

between you and the customer so that you can refer to these in future contacts, or in assessing the value of the customer?

Dealer/distributor information

☐ Basic company information. _____
Do you have complete information on your dealers and distributors as an organisation, including business history, credit checks, banking references, etc?

☐ Personal data. _____
Do you have complete information on the key people – not only the principals, but also the sales people, so that you can contact them personally for an incentive activity.

☐ History of relationship. _____
Can you easily trace the flow of (interactive) communications between you and the dealer so that you can refer to these in future contacts, or in assessing the value of the dealer/distributor?

☐ Allocated sales leads and results. _____
Do you register which leads you provide to your dealers and distributors, and their performance in converting the leads to solid prospects and customers?

☐ Sales achievements. _____
Can you easily assess how your dealers and distributors are performing for you?

Sales force information

☐ Basic personal information. _____
Do you have current data and background information on all your salespeople, including the phone numbers to ring when they are unreachable?

☐ Assigned clients. _____
Can you readily see which customers and prospects are handled by which salespeople?

☐ Allocated sales leads and results. _____
Do you register which leads you provide to your sales force –

and their performance in converting the leads to solid prospects and customers?

☐ Sales cycle reporting. _____
Can you quickly determine how each salesperson is progressing in his/her efforts to convert a prospect into a customer? Do you have, or need, mileposts in your sales cycle, with probability scores assigned to each step?

☐ Time accounting. _____
Can you – and the salesperson – see where and how he/she has been spending his/her time?

☐ Action planning. _____
Do you register specific activities planned for each salesperson for each account, ie visit, call for demonstration, send a business letter, etc?

☐ Sales results. _____
Does your system track sales results for each salesperson, including customer scores, ie changes in either customer status and/or prospect status caused by the salesperson?

Product information

☐ Your products and services. _____
Does your system contain data on all your products: make, models, serial numbers, prices, etc?

☐ Your competitors' products and services. _____
And similar information on key products and services of your competitors?

Marketing activities information

☐ Types of activity. _____
Does your system register all marketing activities, categorised by type, ie direct mail, response advertisement, sweepstake action, product seminar, etc.

☐ Objectives/forecast._____
Do you specify the objectives for each marketing activity – and forecast results?

☐ Specific media and lists employed. _____
Can your system recall the media and/or lists employed for
the activity so that you can use them again if they are winners
– or drop them if they turn out to be losers?

☐ Offer made. _____
Or the offer – the specific proposition designed to stimulate
response so that you can use it again if it is a winner, or drop it
if it is a loser?

Your Customer Marketing System

Good customer marketing information is necessary. But so is a system to store, manage and analyse the information while providing tools for personalised communications.

Theoretically, your customer marketing system can be a simple card file. But with powerful personal computers costing only a few pounds a day on a lease basis, it makes sense to use one.

The basic customer marketing system structure has at its centre, of course, the customer database, with sub–databases on the sales force, marketing activities, dealers (if relevant) and products.

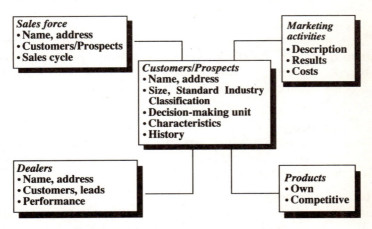

Figure 38 *Basic customer marketing system*

How do you rate your customer marketing system? Check it out!

+	=	Good
0	=	So-so
−	=	Poor
?	=	You don't know at this moment
NA	=	The item is not applicable to your organisation

Information storage and management

☐ User-friendly.
Do you need to be a rocket scientist to work with your system? Or does even the least adept salesperson discover that he/she can make call reports with the system better and faster than with pen and paper?

☐ Flexible.
Can you quickly adapt the system to meet changes in your markets and products? Or do you have to wait six months before somebody can find time to write a new program?

☐ Effective.
Does your system have the power and capacity to do all the tasks you want it to do now – and in the future?

Communications

☐ Mailings.
Can you easily send personalised mailings to prospects and customers? Which refer to your relationship (products purchased, requests for information, etc)? Look like normal correspondence (some computer systems output only in capital letters)?

☐ Telemarketing.
Does your system produce lists with telephone numbers? Can you put a telemarketing script on your computer screen so that the operator can immediately input data?

☐ Refined selections.
Can you make refined selections from your database such as: 'all customers who have spent more than £500 in the past six months, have been customers for more than three years and live within 30 miles of the store'?

Analysis

☐ Sales forecasting.
Can your system produce sales forecasts per period, per product, per salesperson, etc?

☐ Customer identification.
Can your system identify your customers, not just by name and address, but also provide an analysis of customers per type and segment?

☐ Who buys what.
Can your system provide an analysis of products/ services purchased by specific customer types and segments? Analysis of products purchased, customer types and segments?

☐ Customer value.
Can your system provide a value for each client, ie turnover and profitability in the past, and some kind of projection for the future?

☐ Who decides, buys and uses our products.
Does your system identify the 'decision-making unit' in a customer organisation – the buyers, the users, the decision makers and the influencers?

☐ Sales force performance.
Does your system help you to see quickly which salespeople are performing on target?

☐ Distribution channels.
Does your system help you to identify quickly which distribution channels and specific dealers/distributors are performing well?

☐ Media, methods and messages.
Can your system quickly turn out an analysis of the effectiveness of key elements of your marketing activities – media, methods, messages, offers, etc?

☐ Return on investment.
Can your system produce information concerning your overall return on investment from your marketing and sales efforts?

Your Customer Marketing Communications

Customer marketing communications are sent out by a company to meet customer goals. As such, they must be carefully planned and targeted at specific individuals to start, maintain or renew an interactive dialogue which leads to a desired – and measurable – result.

How do you rate your customer marketing communications? Check it out!

+   = Good
0   = So-so
–   = Poor
?   = You don't know at this moment
NA = The item is not applicable to your organisation

☐ Personalised.
Do your communications address an individual by name? Do they appeal to his/her known needs and interests?

☐ Interactive.
Do your communications ask for some kind of response – and make that response easy through, for instance, a pre-addressed, postage-paid reply card?

☐ Benefit orientated.
Do your communications stress specific benefits that the customer or prospect will enjoy if he/she responds?

☐ Customer-orientated.
Are your routine communications (invoices, instructions, product information, etc) written for the intended receiver – or for the convenience of the sender?

Check Your Results

Go back and look at your scores and add them up.

- Do you have lots of +'s?
  Congratulations! You have a well–oiled customer marketing operation in place.

- Do you have lots of 0's?
  Why not talk to the people in the areas where there are some weaknesses to get ideas for improvement.

- Lots of −'s?
  Better make a customer marketing action plan, or accept the fact that you simply won't have a customer-orientated organisation.

- Lots of ?'s?
  Make it a point to find out these answers. Give yourself a deadline.

- Lots of NA's?
  You should really ask yourself again – 'What business am I in?'

A final suggestion: if you want to implement customer marketing in your own company, don't try to do it all at once throughout the organisation.

Start with a 'pilot project' in a small unit where you know people will be enthusiastic about trying it out, and where you are pretty sure it will be successful. Then let the pilot project participants be your ambassadors for selling the idea of customer marketing in other business units.

Further Reading from Kogan Page

Commonsense Direct Marketing, 2nd edition, Drayton Bird
Customer Service, Malcolm Peel
The Effective Use of Market Research, 2nd edition, Robin Birn
A Handbook of Sales and Marketing Management, Len Rogers
Handbook of Telemarketing, Michael Stevens
How to Market Books, Alison Baverstock
The Industrial Market Research Handbook, 2nd edition,
    Paul N Hague
Multi-Level Marketing, Peter Clothier
Practical Marketing, David H Bangs
Researching Business Markets, Ken Sutherland
Total Quality Marketing, John Fraser-Robinson
Understanding Brands, Don Cowley

Sales

The Best Seller, Ley D Forbes
Cold Calling Techniques, Stephan Schiffman
How to Increase Sales Without Leaving Your Desk, Edmund Tirbutt
The Sales Professional, David Mercer
Selling to Win, Richard Denny

A full list of Kogan Page business books is available from the publishers at 120 Pentonville Road, London N1 9JN.